THE LORD IS MY JOY

PAUL DE JAEGHER, S.J.

The Lord
is my
Joy

THE NEWMAN PRESS
WESTMINSTER, MARYLAND
1949

CONTENTS

PART III. MARY AND THE SAINTS

PART IV. THE VIRTUES

PREFACE

GOD, infinite love, is infinitely prodigal of Himself. *Amor diffusus est sui*. He has an immense desire to communicate to us some share of His divine perfections. All the beauty, love, wisdom and holiness in the world are but a drop spilt from the ocean of the divine perfections.

But perhaps we too often forget that God is also supreme happiness. In contemplating His divine perfection He experiences intense delight and infinite joy. As with His other perfections, He bestows this happiness in some measure on us His creatures whom He loves so much. Infinitely happy, He takes pleasure in making us happy too. All the joy and happiness of this world come from Him, the ocean of infinite beatitude.

Alas, He is very far from being able to make us as happy as He would like to. He can only give us His bliss, like His other perfections, according to our capacity, which is very slight, and depends on our dispositions, above all on our generosity. The emptier we are of self and self-love, and the more we open our hearts, the greater the measure in which we receive the precious balm of the divine perfections and, consequently, the divine happiness.

This comes to the same thing as saying that the more faithful a soul is to grace and union with God, the more she shares in His holiness, His love and His joy. Our happiness increases with our union with God, with our holiness. The soul that is in closest communion with God, the soul in which Christ lives most fully and sheds the influence of His ineffable virtues, is also the soul which most tastes the heavenly joys which Jesus experiences in the loving contemplation of His Father's perfections, not only by Himself, but by all His mystical members in whom He lives.

The holiest soul is therefore the happiest, however paradoxical that may seem. No one was ever as happy as the virgin of Nazareth. Not that such a soul is secure from suffering. Far from it. But having found the secret of how to love suffering, the soul knows how to extract a sweet joy from it.

*   *   *   *

It is this aspect of the spiritual life that we wish to display in these pages, by indicating the holy and spiritual joy that is experienced by the happiest souls, those who have attained the life of union.

Worldly people usually imagine that the spiritual life is gloomy, that souls consecrated to God have renounced happiness and the joy of loving. If they were to read these pages they would see how mistaken they are. It is not for them, however, that we write. Even among fervent souls there are too many who let themselves be rather frightened by the painful and austere side of the interior life, by the sufferings that an increasingly perfect life of abnegation involves. They are not sufficiently conscious that the more one loves God with pure love, the more one feels, in Jesus and with Jesus, that spiritual joy, gift of the Holy Ghost, which is the very fruit of love. In this way the soul comes to find real happiness in the very abnegation in which others see practically nothing but pain.

It is good for our zest in the spiritual life not to lose sight of its attractive side, which is real, though little understood. Hilarem datorem diligit Deus—God loves a cheerful giver.

This book is addressed in the first place to souls that have reached the life of Union. No doubt the Holy

Spirit, who is their master and guide, leads them where He will. Their prayer is very simple and mainly passive. They have long lost both the taste and the capacity for meditation, reasoning on a given subject. But these souls too have their hours of aridity, sometimes years of very painful spiritual dryness. At such times it is good for them, on occasion, and according to their inclination, to use a book that suggests sentiments in keeping with the unitive life, and in harmony with those they feel in their own hearts. By doing this they would be following the advice of the great contemplative of Avila, who advised even souls who have reached the summits of the mystical life to use sometimes the twigs of affectionate thoughts to re-kindle the fire smouldering in their hearts.

Nevertheless we write above all for souls who, having passed generously through the purgative way, are briskly advancing in the illuminative way, and approaching the life of Union to which they aspire, the threshold of which they may already have reached. May this sketch of these joys, many of which will be new to them or at least untasted in their full intensity, open out new horizons for such souls. Perhaps it will do more. It will gradually make them familiar with the sentiment of self-forgetfulness in very pure love of God, which is characteristic of the unitive way. Nothing could prepare them better for such a noble life, to which all their desires tend.

*   *   *   *

We have written these pages despite the absorbing and very varied occupations of a missionary's life. The motive that has chiefly inspired us is that, in the author's opinion, this aspect of the spiritual life has been very little stressed, and the higher joys of love have not been described, at least not methodically. No doubt the writings of the

saints and especially of the great mystics—St. Teresa of
Avila, St. John of the Cross, Angela of Foligno, Veronica
Giuliani—are full of ardent expressions that reveal their
overflowing happiness. But they do not treat of spiritual
joy systematically. Hence it is a good thing to group the
sentiments and joys proper to the life of Union, to display their source, and to suggest the thoughts that
generate them. More than one soul will perhaps learn in
this way to experience for the first time this or that sentiment proper to the unitive life, which will be the
precious source of excellent acts of very pure love.

Some people, perhaps, will reproach us with giving a
false picture of the interior life by listing exclusively its
spiritual joys, instead of showing it in its true light, with
its suffering and troubles as well as its delights and consolations. We are not unaware of, nor do we wish to hide,
the painful side of the spiritual life. We know very well
that the interior life is in no way an uninterrupted series
of delightful joys. We know, as our readers do, that
Christ invited us to take up our cross daily and follow
Him, and that, according to the Apostle of the Gentiles,
we must make up in us what is wanting to the passion of
Christ.

But we were free to choose, among the various aspects
of the interior life, one aspect that had not perhaps been
sufficiently stressed. Much has been written on suffering,
its beauty and apostolic value, on compassion for Christ
Crucified, on the life of sacrifice. Less has been written
on spiritual joy. Yet spiritual suffering and spiritual joy,
both springing from perfect love, are two excellent sentiments of a Christian soul, two magnificent flowers that
must be carefully cultivated in the garden of the Church.

St. Ignatius, in his immortal book of Spiritual Exercises, devotes the whole of the third week to compassion

for the sufferings of Christ. Then, leading us higher still, he teaches us during the whole of the fourth and last week to share the joys of our glorified Saviour. The marvellous meditation to obtain the love of God, which crowns his Exercises, is nothing else but the final rung of the ladder that should raise us to the spiritual and loving joy experienced by the soul that contemplates God's love, and His other perfections.

Now it is precisely this spiritual joy, to which St. Ignatius, that great master of the spiritual life, attached so much importance, and which is so noble, for it is nothing else than sharing in God's own joy, that we have tried to describe. It therefore was no part of our plan to speak at length of suffering, except when opportunity occurred to show that sufferings themselves change for the loving soul into divine joys. Is it not one of the greatest triumphs of Christian piety to make the roses of joy blossom among the thorns of suffering?

Others, perhaps, will judge that though we imagine we have avoided spiritual egotism, we are in fact nourishing it by offering the soul a whole series of joys, each sweeter than the last. Not only however do many of these joys not belong to the sensible order, but it must not be forgotten that those we mention are almost exclusively joys of a very disinterested love, and pre-suppose a great forgetfulness of self. A selfish soul could never experience them. Besides, however spiritual and holy they may be, we in no way propose them for their own sake, but for the sake of the very pure love of which they are the exquisite flower. Anyone who tried to seek them for the mere sake of enjoyment would never attain them.

*   *   *   *

Is it necessary to state that we have no illusions about

this sketch of the nobler joys of the life of Union? It will
necessarily be very imperfect. The saints themselves,
despite the vivid experience they had of them, often only
succeeded in stammering. Even more frequently they
preferred to remain silent, not finding any adequate expression in our poor human language. The fact is that
these divine joys are all the more spiritual and simple, and
therefore more difficult to express, in proportion as the
soul becomes more united to God, and more simple in
herself. Besides they are more a question of affection and
experience than of the understanding. They are tasted
rather than expressed. It would be very difficult to put
into words the flavour of a peach, a strawberry or a
cherry, above all to someone who had never tasted them.
All we can hope to try to do is to supply the themes of
unitive meditations, indicate the beauty of such and such
a sentiment, and show how fit it is to blossom out into
holy jubilation. We can certainly point out from a
distance the delectable fruits of spiritual joy. God alone,
by His graces, whether mystical or not, can place them in
our hands, and make us taste and relish them.

What adds even more to the difficulty of our task is
that these joys, though apparently very varied, all resemble one another to some extent. They are all unitive
joys, joys of communion with the Beloved. All of them
centre in the unique and fundamental joy: that of living
in union with Jesus, by perfect love, in God; that of losing
and forgetting oneself in Him, in order to espouse His interests and His happiness; of enjoying in Him His divine
perfections that have become our own. How often we
shall have to return to this essential joy. It will be our
leitmotif throughout these pages. The reader will surely
excuse us if we are driven to repeat ourselves more than
once.

Is it necessary to add, in conclusion, that we do not claim to describe all the joys of the life of union? Far from it. We have merely chosen those which many souls seem to be unaware of, yet which are characteristic of the unitive life. Even so we have selected only a few of these splendid joys.

"A soul cannot approach My Heart without being happy, for I am the source of joy and happiness. Even in moments when I associate a soul most intimately with My Passion and sufferings, I know how to change all bitterness into sweetness. I keep you in My Heart and in the depths of the essence of the Most Holy Trinity. I therefore wish you to be happy, as I am, even now, in the measure in which you suffer with Me, in proportion to your love for Me and the consolation you give Me. Perfect and constant joy in Me is the greatest proof of perfect and constant union with Me. You love Me sincerely. It is I who act in you and by you. I therefore wish to prove it by the radiance of My divine joy.

"Souls are only unhappy to the extent in which they withdraw from God. The great desire of My Father, and My own, would be to see every soul happy, even on earth. When divine justice imposes affliction, or punishes, it is always out of love, in order to bring souls nearer to God, their sovereign good. My spouse, work with Me to make souls happy." [1]

---

[1] Words of our Saviour to Marie St. Cecilia of Rome. See, *Une vie dans le Christ*, the autobiography of Marie St. Cecilia (Dina Bélanger), nun of Jésus-Marie (1897-1929), 2 vols. Couvent de Jésus-Marie, Sillery, P.Q., Canada, 1934. Numerous fine passages on spiritual joy will be found in this life of the Canadian mystic. Cf. vol. 2, pp. 90; 239-240; 241-242; 303, etc. Marie St. Cecilia can truly be called the messenger of joy in divine love and of happiness in suffering.

I. WHY THIS INTRODUCTION TO THE JOYS OF
THE UNITIVE LIFE?

In these pages we have above all tried to sketch—it is all we could hope to do—the exquisite joys of souls who have attained the unitive life. Joys that consist entirely of love, and which are in reality the joy of Jesus Himself in the soul. Joys experienced in admiring and loving, in union with Him, all the perfections of God, of Mary and the saints. Joys of a very unitive kind, which presuppose a very disinterested love, and make us live in God and enjoy His good as our own.

These joys are little known to many fervent souls, sometimes entirely unsuspected by them. By revealing these joys to them, therefore, we hope to give them a glimpse of the domain of sanctity, and inflame their desire of climbing higher. Excelsior!

Too many generous souls, we must admit, stop half-way on the road to sanctity. What is it they lack? No doubt the great obstacle is usually want of generosity. But it is often the fact that they have not the remotest idea of what the sentiments of the unitive life and of perfect love are. Therefore they prepare badly. They are held up in what we might call the negative part of the spiritual life. They restrict themselves to thoughts and affections suitable to the purgative or illuminative ways, almost exclusively directed to correcting their faults. Instead of stopping there, they ought to look higher, accustom themselves to enjoying the happiness of living in God, and make themselves familiar with the sentiments of very pure love, which belong to the unitive life and sanctity.

*   *   *   *

Another aim we have had in mind is to invite souls to come out of themselves. One of the great obstacles to the unitive life in fact is the spiritual egotism from which many souls imprisoned within themselves unwittingly suffer. They are too busy analysing themselves or lamenting their ills. Not knowing how to lose sight of self, they remain almost completely unaware of the splendid joys of the unitive life of perfect love. They never, or scarcely ever, think of rejoicing at the perfections of God (whom nevertheless they love sincerely) or of finding their happiness in the immense felicity which is His. Yet is it not a characteristic of love, of authentic, pure love, to make us live as it were in those we love, to make us find our happiness in them, to take pride and pleasure in them? Therefore to teach souls to forget themselves in God, to identify themselves with Him, to share His joys and those of the Blessed Virgin, our Mother, and the saints, our heavenly brothers and sisters, is surely to teach them at the same time to love much more, and in a much more excellent way.

* * * *

By doing that we should achieve a third object, that of teaching loving souls to enlarge immeasurably too cramped a spiritual life and to enrich themselves with all the wealth of God Himself. Why do so many souls grieve over their faults and their poverty in a way that depresses them? Because they live too much within themselves. It is precisely the egotism which we have already mentioned, inherent in their spiritual outlook, that makes them possess only what is strictly and individually their own. But pure love, unitive love, dilates the heart in a remarkable way, and enriches us unbelievably. If we have

such love, all that we love is ours. Such love gives us all
the good things, the perfections and the happiness of
those dear to us. All those things become our own. We
enjoy them as if they were a personal possession.

May the souls who meditate on these thoughts of
unitive love grow fully, that they may learn to be happy
with an immense happiness, happy with all the infinite
happiness of heaven and earth.

That is the true sense of the wonderful Communion of
Saints, which so few realise or appreciate in its magnificent beauty.

That is also what our beatitude will be in heaven. It
will not consist in an egotistical enjoyment of heavenly
goods, far from it. The perfections of God, of Jesus,
Mary, the angels and the saints, their felicity of love,
their holiness, their glory, will be our whole happiness.
We will rejoice and live therein much more than in our
own. In reality our own felicity will be immense, con-
stituted as it will be by our sharing in all their happiness
and perfections, much more than by enjoying merely our
own personal beatitude. The latter will seem a mere
speck in comparison.

Since our life here below is a slow journey to our
heavenly country, should we not begin even now to prepare for the sentiments and thoughts of heaven? Or are
we going to remain until death strangers to all the exquisite sentiments of perfect love and the most holy joys
which will fill our eternity?

2. THE JOY OF LOVING

1. God in His supreme goodness has not kept for Himself the immense happiness that is His. From the limitless

ocean of infinite beatitude He has shed a few drops on us, His beloved children. The joys He has thus scattered in this world are endlessly varied.

Of all these joys, the finest, the sweetest, the dearest, is certainly the joy of loving. This is the queen of joys. Remove it and the earth would be cold, dull, sunless.

2. But what precisely is this mysterious thing that God has implanted in every human heart, which we call love? It would be very hard to define it perfectly. No matter, we all know by experience what it is to love. We have all felt the intimate joy that love produces and of which St. Augustine well said "Amor sibi ipsi praemium, love is its own reward".

No doubt love and the joy of loving have many forms and many degrees, according to their object. In the wide sense of the word the artist loves, and knows the joy of loving, when he contemplates admiringly the work his genius has produced. The scientist also loves when he passionately carries forward his experiments that may revolutionise the world. The tourist in search of grandiose views and beautiful places also loves and takes delight in gazing at the beauty of nature.

3. But even taken in its stricter sense of affection for another person, love assumes many forms and has many degrees. The friend who takes his friend's arm and confides in him knows the happiness of loving. Greater still is the joy of loving that fills a mother when with delight she kisses her baby, or when she sees around her the children who are a part of herself, her happiness and crown. Above all there is the joy of the deep love that joins two lives in one, the joy of married people.

Yet it is above all spiritual love, the love of God, that makes known the finest joys of loving. This is not surprising. Here there are none of the imperfections or faults which in this world always limit and often spoil the lovableness of the person we love. God is lovable beyond all possibility of love. We can never love Him enough. Knowing that gives our love wings and begets joys that the world does not even suspect to exist. What more delightful for the truly loving soul than to think that the God whom she loves is infinitely perfect, infinitely lovable?

This joy, this ecstasy of loving with one's whole soul a God whose attractions surpass a thousand times those of the world, is often experienced even by a soul that is only beginning the spiritual life. The spiritual consolations that God sends such a soul amply compensate the sacrifices she makes for Him. But this joy increases concurrently with the love of God. Then a moment comes when the soul, giving herself entirely to God, chooses the King of Kings as her spouse, and becomes herself in a way a queen of the universe. Finally and above all, there is the ardent love and perfect joy in loving of the saint, who has entirely abandoned self, and, rising above the petty joys of this earth and aspiring ever higher, has established his abode among the divine perfections, in which at certain times he loses himself in an ecstasy of love. It is the saint above all who knows the deep and as it were divine joy of loving.

4. The purer the love, in fact, the purer the joy of loving. The closer love resembles the divine love whence it flows, the more beautiful and divine is the joy of loving, and the more exactly does it mirror the infinitely beatific joy with which God loves Himself, the infinitely lovable, in the Trinity of His persons.

The ecstasy to which this joy of loving can lead is known, not, alas, from our own personal experience, but by the sublime exclamations it called forth from the great mystics. "Ah," said St. Mary Magdalen of Pazzi, "if a single drop of what I feel in my heart were to fall into hell, hell would at once become heaven." St. John of the Cross, lost in the entrancing contemplation of the God he loved, exclaimed, "If you had seen a ray of the glory of my Beloved, you would endure a thousand deaths to see it again, and having seen it again, you would want to die again in order to see it once more".

We all know the joy of loving, but there are few souls, very few souls, who know the higher kinds of this joy. Our love is too impure, too mingled with egotism. Our joy in loving suffers by this lack of purity.

That is true not only of human love but also of the love of many souls consecrated to God. Even the spiritual consolations that they enjoy at certain times, even perhaps the mystical joys that God grants them gratuitously, out of pure liberality, are not pure enough, not disinterested enough. The soul is often attached to them, perhaps without realising it, or unwittingly finds therein a secret self-satisfaction.

Authentically pure and holy joy begins above all when a soul has given herself entirely to God, left self to live in God. These are the joys of union, joys of a definitely unitive kind. They are joys that the soul only experiences because she shares by unitive love and the unitive life in all the perfections of God, whom she loves. By admiration and loving delight she possesses and enjoys them, as if those perfections were really her own. A self-centred soul evidently could not know such joys.

5. If we analyse this thought more deeply and seek the ultimate reason for these higher joys, what makes them possible, we discover that these pure delights are the joys of a soul intimately united to Jesus, identified with Him. They are the joys that Jesus Himself lives in the soul.

"Vivo, jam non ego, vivit vero in me Christus." It is
Jesus who lives in the soul and with unutterable bliss
contemplates in her and by her, the bewitching perfections of His beloved Father. It is Jesus who irradiates the
soul with His charity, who loves His Father in her to the
point of ecstasy, and whose beatifying love fills the soul.
In Jesus and by Jesus she can say in all truth and with
great happiness, "Deus meus et omnia. Oh beloved
Father, You are indeed mine, and You are everything to
me." Jesus living, loving, and possessing His Father in
her and by her, such is the ultimate secret of these
unitive and most pure joys.

It is above all these unitive joys that we have tried to
sketch in these pages. Do you also wish, generous soul,
to know these joys? Leave self. Come forth from the
prison of your egotism, above all your spiritual egotism
that walls you up within narrow, dark limits. Give yourself without reserve to Jesus so that He may live in you
His own noble joys. Soon He will make you feel what
perhaps you have never before experienced. He will
widen your heart, He will dilate it immensely. His pure
love infused within you will replace the petty self-
centred joys that you delighted in by infinitely nobler
and sweeter joys, joys immense in scope, the unitive joys
of pure love, His own joys.

3.   VARIETY OF THE JOYS OF LOVE

1. We have seen that the more closely a soul approaches
and resembles God, the more she shares in His divine
perfections and happiness, experiencing more and more
sublime joys.

Does this mean that perfect souls, saints especially, are always filled with ecstatic joy? Far from it.

In the first place it is true that the more perfect a soul, the more perfect the joy experienced, at least at certain times. But it does not follow that such souls always enjoy these ineffable delights. It would be too dangerous for the soul to be always filled with such happiness. There would be too much risk of becoming attached to it, besides, the soul would already be receiving her reward in this life, and her love would suffer as a consequence. The cross, which is perhaps her chief sustenance, would no longer play a sufficient part in her life. God prefers to alternate joys and sorrows, consolations and aridity, according to a measure which His divine wisdom varies for each one of us.

2. Furthermore, one must not forget that there are many ways of loving God, and likewise many ways of knowing the joy of loving Him.

Sometimes, especially at the beginning, joy fills the soul like a spring gaily bubbling on the ground. The soul that has only recently devoted herself to the interior life is very happy through the divine consolations she feels, and their sweetness exceeds any merely human joy.

Sometimes, above all in more advanced souls, joy leaps like a waterfall. The soul is exultant, transported with happiness at the thought of the love of God and His divine lovableness, and bursts forth in ardent prayers and loving affections.

Sometimes, chiefly in perfect souls, joy flows gently, like a great river whose current is almost imperceptible. It is a deep joy, hidden in the centre of the soul, wholly spiritual and interior. The soul scarcely feels any need of telling God of her happiness, but silently and peacefully enjoys the presence or perfections of the Beloved.

3. Finally we must also and above all distinguish between sensible joy and joy which is not emotional. All the intermediate degrees must also be taken into consideration.

At the beginning of the spiritual life consolations are intended chiefly to detach the soul from all earthly satisfactions. But as the soul is still very dependent on the senses, she is scarcely capable of the higher, spiritual joys. The palate is not yet sufficiently sensitive. And so God adapts His consolations to the soul's condition, bestowing joys of a less refined, more emotional kind, in which the senses have a large share.

In proportion to the soul's progress, however, her joys become less emotional. A soul that has passed through the long dryness and painful purification of the Dark Night of the Senses, and still more a soul that has been a prey to the torturing anguish of the Night of the Soul, experiences subsequently very pure and sublime spiritual delights, in which the senses usually have no part. The source of happiness is then the depth and centre of the soul, where God Himself produces infused passive love with the joy that is, as it were, its flower.

This does not prevent these purely spiritual joys from affecting sometimes the inferior powers of our being. They are sometimes so intense and abundant that they overflow the soul and fill the senses, which share in them, though actually in a different and more subtle way than in the decidedly emotional delights of the beginner.

4. Perfect souls often feel this happiness in the form of a very simple, calm peace. This is the peace that St. Teresa of the Child Jesus, even though she was so detached from divine consolations, did not hesitate to ask of God, when she said, "Jesus, I ask you for only one thing, peace, and above all, love".

A deep peace, unshakable, because founded on the

changeless perfections of God. A soul wholly united to God is continually aware that her Beloved is infinitely perfect, and unutterably happy in the enjoyment of His divine perfections. This awareness is scarcely ever absent, and gradually gives the soul as it were a well of happiness, of which human vicissitudes and the most painful sufferings can do no more than ruffle the surface.

Yet this happiness itself may assume a non-emotional form, dry and tasteless. This is what happens, for example, during periods of prolonged aridity, or when the soul is suffering the passive purifications by which God leads to the heights of divine union. Despite everything, the soul retains the memory of the delights experienced in moments of divine visitation. She knows that she herself may be tossed unceasingly by the waves of spiritual change, but that God, her all-in-all, continues to enjoy with unchangeable felicity His divine perfections. God her Beloved is happy. That is sufficient for her, too, to be always happy and contented.

5. In the following chapters we will pass in review a few of the very varied delights experienced by souls that have attained the unitive life. The delights engendered by the thought of the divine lovableness; by being as it were lost in God; by being able to love Him unceasingly; the delight of causing Jesus joy; the joy Mary and the saints give us; delight in the virtues.

Do not, however, imagine, soul whom Jesus loves, that all who live the unitive life equally experience *all* these delights. God's grace is infinitely varied and takes into account differences of temperament and tastes. At will, it enlightens us to appreciate and take pleasure now in this truth, now in another. One soul, perhaps, will habitually feel happiness in the divine perfections that she considers as hers, while not knowing the delights of the Eucharist

or the joy of sharing in the Passion of Jesus. Another
soul will frequently be delighted at the thought that she
is the tabernacle of Jesus Christ, yet will never experience the mysterious joy of despising self, of feeling small,
that the Saint of Lisieux knew so well.

Do not forget that it is one thing to understand a truth
by faith and reasoning, another vividly to realise and
appreciate it, with the help of a special grace, perhaps
even a mystical grace of infused enlightenment and
passive love.

You, perhaps, have discovered this for yourself at some
time. As a child you knew quite well that Mary was your
mother but you did not live by this truth; it was not your
joy and delight. One day perhaps Mary mysteriously
came nearer to you and as it were pressed you to her
motherly heart, filling you with happiness of a new kind.
That day Mary became for you a real mother. Of course
the ardent insight and blissful love of that moment are
long since passed and gone. Yet the perfume of that
precious grace has remained. Have you not felt since
then for Mary a child's love, unknown to you before? A
great grace, quite gratuitous, that Mary obtained for you
out of motherly kindness, one that changed your whole
life, establishing you permanently in a relation of
intimate filial familiarity with her.

6. How precious a grace to have experienced sometimes,
or even once, the great and exquisite joys of love that
belong to the unitive life. Even only once to have loved
as one's own, blissfully, the beauty, love, purity and
happiness of God! To have felt, if only once, the happiness of being plunged in that ocean of Love! To have
known by experience the proud honour of being the
spouse of Jesus and queen of the universe, or to have
rested with delight on Mary's breast like a favourite

child.　Splendid joys, precious graces that re-echo throughout our lives, thanks to which we can often re-live to some extent, even in aridity, those pure and noble sentiments, and which will help us to come out of ourselves more and more in order to lose ourselves in God, our treasure.　One can say without hesitation that these intense and pure joys, gifts of divine liberality, are the fine pearls and jewels of our spiritual life.

May God in His merciful love multiply them for my readers, and give them the opportunity to find some new delight, unknown to them before, that will open new vistas and be an abundant source of new acts of most pure love.

Like a diligent bee, go gathering now the honey of divine joys that these pages indicate to you.　The flowers that blossom there are infinitely various.　Some will certainly seem closed at first, charming buds, pleasant to look at, but not a source of nectar.　One day you will notice them again.　Some generous act of yours, a cross borne with love or, most often of all, Jesus' pure liberality will, like a warm ray of sunshine, have caused these flowers to open.　You will find in them happiness in an ecstasy of love.

PART I. GOD

4. JOY IN OUR SUBLIME DESTINY

1. God freely and lovingly created us to know Him, love Him and serve Him in this world and thus merit the eternal and perfect happiness of heaven. A truth that every Christian learns in childhood, and which is the foundation of our whole spiritual life.

There are, however, many ways of interpreting this great truth. For most of the faithful, God is above all the great King, the Supreme Master of the World, and His love for us is a love of kindness, compassion and benevolence towards all His subjects, His puny creatures. In His merciful love for us, He even sacrificed His Only Son. Why? To save at one stroke, by a supreme device, the whole human race from hell, terrible and eternal.

Yet in proportion as one advances in the spiritual life, one gradually comes to understand that God's love is more than a general love that comprises everybody indistinctly, more than a benevolent love. It is a friend's love, a very personal love. A person to whom Our Lord confides secrets in the intimacy of his heart comes to realise that God loves him personally, that He died for him, that He desires *his* love and is always thinking of *him*. "Dilexit me et tradidit semetipsum pro me—He loved *me* and delivered Himself for *me*" (Gal. ii.20).

Then, as divine light and God's loving kindnesses in the depths of the heart keep increasing, the soul begins to perceive that God loves her, not merely with a very personal love, but with a most perfect love, with unitive love. Soon she sees that God is really in love with her, that He desires to give Himself entirely, and expects from her a perfect love in return. Even in this life He wants to be united to the soul very intimately, as a prelude to the perfect and eternal union of the beatific vision.

2. God therefore desires to be united to me. He created me for that purpose, towards which all His efforts and all His mysterious activities on this earth converge. He desires union, as all lovers do. The union of married people is merely a distant pale reflection of the close union that God desires to contract with me even in this life, by holiness. "Sponsabo te in fide—I shall expouse thee in faith" (Osee ii. 20).

A strange mystery, that seems absurd, mad, to worldly people. What, the great God who created and maintains every instant the whole universe by one eternal thought, the King of Kings, Lord of time and eternity, is in love with His puny creature, a beggar in rags, and dreams of being intimately united to her! If she were even beautiful, with many charming qualities! On the contrary, He loves the repulsive creature that is me, that each of us is, full of every kind of wretchedness, stricken with leprosy and ulcers.

· Is such loving folly possible to God? It is the truth nevertheless. The union of all and nothingness, of infinite holiness and infinite misery, such is the masterpiece that the infinitely condescending and incomprehensible love of God has imagined and wants to create. He created me solely for this union, He predestined me for it. All the events that His providence arranges, all the spiritual graces He gives me, all the desolation and consolation He sends me, have no other purpose.

My life is a drama of love, the drama of divine love, that desires union with me, seeks unceasingly and begs

for my heart, pursues me tirelessly with love, and strives
to win me by innumerable gifts of all kinds.

3. What are these gifts of my divine Lover? They are as
marvellous as His love itself.

My body; my soul with its noble powers, above all
sanctifying grace which makes it infinitely beautiful even
in the sight of God Himself, and in a certain fashion
divinizes it; the gift of pious parents; the grace of a
Christian education; a vocation to the priesthood or the
religious life, with all the special spiritual graces that it
implies; God's continual tokens of affection towards me;
all these things are gifts from God's unitive love, gifts He
bestows on me to induce me to love Him.

Then around me all the creatures, animate and in-
animate, which nourish me, give me pleasure, or are useful to me, the whole world itself is a present from Him.
God creates and conserves the universe for me, to show
me His love! Even the great sun that gives life and light
to the world, even the moon and the innumerable hosts
of stars were made for me, for love of me. They are all
presents, jewels finely set, diamonds and pearls of price,
gifts of His love. How wonderful and enviable is my lot!
No princess in the world was ever showered with such
gifts by her royal fiancé.

4. How does my royal Beloved send me the innumerable
gifts that He unceasingly makes me? Does He send them
by messenger? No, He knows that they will please me
more if He hands them to me personally, so that is what
He does.

It is well to note: God Himself is present in each of
His gifts. He fills the whole world. In each flower, fruit,
insect, He is present. He is hidden in them and speaks—
"Beloved soul, see how I love you. I am in this flower
and make it beautiful to please you, because I love you. I

am in this fruit and make it agreeable for your pleasure. This butterfly hides Me, and I make it graceful and gay for your diversion. Love Me as I love you.''

That is why so many saints loved nature so much. With the eyes of living faith and ardent love they saw in nature the God who is hidden and yet reveals Himself therein. They discovered in nature God begging for our affection. At the sight of a rose St. Ignatius was inflamed with love. St. John of the Cross, that great lover of nature, often used to leave his monastery to plunge into the solitude of flower-covered hills and wooded mountains, passing days and even whole nights there in loving contemplation.

5. But God, in His loving desire for union, does even more to win my heart. All who love try to make known their attractive qualities in order to please the person they love. That is their great means of winning affection.

Will not God, the lover par excellence, do the same thing? Will He not show His face and conquer my heart by the splendour of His divine beauty?

That is in fact what He does. He shows Himself, makes Himself known to me. Alas, it must be confessed that He cannot do so as much as He would like to. His greatness itself and the brilliance of His divine perfections put a certain obstacle in the way.

If He were to show His face unveiled to me, weak creature that I am, my soul would be so fascinated and so irresistibly attracted to Him, that the bonds of this mortal body would break in my flight to the Divine embrace. Therefore He cannot unveil Himself before me in all His splendour. The rays of divine love and divine perfection are too brilliant, too blinding. They would burn the eyes of my soul. God is obliged to diffuse and soften His too powerful radiance, and show Himself to me under the veil of His creatures.

He shows me some reflection of His wisdom and omnipotence in nature, so many of whose wonders are known, but which still hides so many secrets. The smallest atom is a world of marvels that astonish the greatest scientists. A mere wisp of moss, a blade of grass, a tiny flower, the smallest things speak as eloquently to us of the divine wisdom and power as the sun and immensity of stars that shine in the night sky.

To win my heart He also shows me something of His immensity in the oceans stretching away out of sight, and even more in the measureless worlds whose distant stars whisper something to us at night.

He manifests His divine beauty to us in the delightful landscapes that nature offers. Wooded hills and flower-covered valleys, with their pleasant streams. Gigantic mountains of eternal snow and flashing glaciers. Or in human beauty, sometimes so attractive, He lets us see a ray of that divine beauty that we could not see in this life without dying of love, and to which we so seldom think of raising our mind.

Similarly with His other innumerable perfections, goodness, mercy, love, justice, happiness, holiness, etc. For our sake, God makes His creatures a reflection of Himself, saying, "All that is only a shadow of My divine attractions. If only I could show Myself to you, how you would love Me!"

6. In order to prove His ardent love and His desire for union, therefore, God showers us with gifts. He presents these gifts in person. He does even more. To make us think of Him, He unveils Himself to some extent by making these gifts a likeness, though an imperfect one, of Himself. That, however, is not all. His tireless love and passionate desire to unite us to Him do not stop there. He gives Himself in person to us.

This is another and unfathomable mystery of infinite
Love. How can the Most High, a pure spirit, who infinitely transcends matter, give Himself to me? How can
He who is invisible to my bodily eyes even show Himself
in person to me? But the loving wisdom of God infinitely surpasses our poor human minds. The mysterious
incarnation of the divine Word has solved this apparently
insoluble problem. Jesus has shown Himself to us in a
body like our own. He gave Himself to us at Bethlehem
in charming human form, smiling to us, stretching out
His arms to us so that, won by His love, we may tenderly
embrace Him.

Thirty years at Nazareth, thirty years of complete gift
of self, a life of perfect forgetfulness of self. Then the
years of His laborious apostolate during which by His
wonderful discourses He reveals to me the sentiments of
His heavenly Father as well as His own, and strives to win
me to Him by the charm of His inimitable virtues.
Finally Golgotha, the supreme gift of Himself, the great
drama of love, the ultimate method He employs to make
me believe in His passionate love and win my heart.

Even that is not all. Even after His cruel death and
glorious ascension into heaven, Jesus still finds a way of
giving Himself to me. In His incomparable love He comes
down from heaven, stoops down to me, even enters my
soul and tells me again of His love. The Eucharist is the
daily visit of Jesus to the poor soul that He loves so much.
It is His union with me, a union much more intimate than
that of married people. It is a life in common, living
together.

This union with Jesus in some mysterious way continues in me. For it feeds the wonderful union of sanctifying grace, nourishes the mystical life of Jesus in my
soul that lasts night and day and never ceases if I so choose.

7. Nimium dilexit me. Yes, He has truly loved me excessively, to the point of folly! No earthly lover ever loved like this. No one ever gave himself as Jesus has given Himself to me. He is indeed the undisputed King of Love. He can say in all truth, "Beloved soul, have I loved you enough? Have I done enough for you, done enough to prove My love? Quid debui ultra facere vineae meae quod non feci? What should I have done for you that I have not done? Do you believe now that, for all My greatness, I nevertheless love you, My weak little creature, as no one ever loved? Give yourself to Me, give Me your soul for which I hunger and thirst."

How shall I answer the great God who begs so eloquently for my heart? To Jesus who asks, "Do you love Me, will you love Me?" I shall reply gladly like the Apostle St. Peter, "Domine, tu omnia nosti, tu scis quia amo te. Yes Lord, You know that I love You sincerely, ardently, that I want always to love You more and more. Have I not renounced for Your sake all the earthly affections on which I had set my heart? Have I not said goodbye for Your sake to my parents and friends and the good things of this world, in order to follow You everywhere? Above all, haven't I given You my life itself, inviting You to live fully in me, giving You my whole being, for You to see with my eyes, speak by my mouth, and above all love with my heart? Do I not dream of being so identified with You that You alone live in me, life of my life, and soul of my soul?

"Yes, Divine Master, my soul, won by Your love, is in love with You too. You are my only treasure, my only good. My joy and sole desire in this life is to please You and make You happy.

"Yes, alas, I do not love You enough. My love is nothing compared to Yours. I am still far from loving as a soul

ought to who is espoused to the great King of Kings, far
from living only for You and by You. Now, however,
that I understand my sublime destiny in this life better,
and the immensity of Your love for me, I will love You
with all the ardour of my soul. Henceforward all that I
come in contact with, all the events that form the texture
of my life, will seem full of Your presence, Your goodness, Your loving wisdom, Your affection for me. In
them I will hear Your gentle voice saying—'Beloved,
give Me your heart.' It is You alone I shall love in them.
I want to live for love of You.''

"My soul, open fully to joy and love, like a flower to
the sun in spring. You have now seen your life in its true
perspective, infinitely beautiful, grand, resplendent with
divine things. It is radiant, attractive. Your lot is the
finest a creature could wish for. You are made for God,
reserved for Him, sealed with His seal. You are the fortunate spouse for whom the King of Kings longs. Give
your heart wholly to loving. From now on you have
nothing else to do in this life. Love with all your heart,
love passionately Him who is irresistibly attractive, in
comparison with whom everything else seems ugly to
you, and whose far-off likeness discovered in creatures
was sufficient until now to delight your heart. Ama et fac
quod vis. Love and do what you please. God asks
nothing else of you!''[1]

[1]*Confiance*, Vol. 2, Chapter 6, page 205.

5. OMNIA MEA TUA SUNT

1. God's action in a generous soul consists essentially in
detaching her from self in order to attach her to Him, in
making the soul die to self in order to live in Him. If He
asks the soul to sacrifice everything, it is in order to lead
her in the end to leave self. God would have achieved
very little if He did not succeed in gradually emptying the
soul of the self-love that is the root of her love of other
things.

2. In order to bring about this gradual renouncement of
self, God chiefly uses spiritual consolations and desolation. Both serve to show the soul what she really is, an
inexhaustible source of sins, or, as St. Ignatius said, a
repulsive abscess endlessly refilling with filth.

Thus, under God's action, the docile soul, who pre-
viously loved self in all things, gradually comes to be so
disgusted with self, so full of contempt for the person
that she formerly esteemed, that it seems impossible to
love self any longer, at least wilfully, deliberately.

This continual detachment is a very painful crisis for
the soul, tearing her as it were from self—a slow and painful death of the old Adam. How many convulsions will
shake the poor soul before the courageous, final decision
to renounce possession of self, self-love, living for self!

3. But God does not leave the soul all alone in this slow
agony. All is not sorrow and suffering. In proportion as
the soul abandons self, God fills her. The slow and cruel
death that penetrates her is also a new birth, the coming
of the fullness of the life of Christ in the soul. Oportet
illum crescere, me autem minui. Christ must increase
and I must decrease.

The life of the merely natural man, self-love, decreases
and Jesus' life increases accordingly. Finally the day

comes when the soul is so disgusted at her wretchedness, so empty of self and of everything else, that she is really poor in every respect, above all poor in self-love. The famous maxim of St. John of the Cross is fulfilled: "To possess all, strive to possess nothing." Reduced to this total and blessed poverty, the soul turns to God with irresistible, intense longing, and cries, "My God, I no longer possess anything, yet I have a heart that desires to love, cannot but love."

God bends down and offers an ineffable exchange: "Give yourself to Me and I will give Myself to you. Give Me your poor soul, give Me your rags and I will give you in exchange My divine riches. I am here, I am yours, I belong to you. Love Me as your own, as your property. Love Me henceforward instead of self, as your new self. I give you all I have, all that I am. I give you My divine perfections, for them to be yours to the extent you choose, so that you may love them as your own, for your admiration, satisfaction, delight and glory. Do with them what you please. They belong to you, for you are Mine and I am yours. Omnia mea tua sunt. All I have is yours."

4. What an admirable exchange God offers the loving soul, whilst at the same time His grace carries it into effect. The soul to whom He speaks in this way is a thousand times blessed. She gives God her wretched self with all its impurity, egotism and imperfections, and in return God gives Himself to her with all His beauty, lovableness, wisdom, all His power, love and infinite happiness. He gives all that, so that the soul may enjoy it as she pleases, as a real personal possession, so that she may love it instead of self, and look upon it as her new self.

5. But isn't that a mere metaphor? Do the divine

treasures really become the soul's own treasures, making her infinitely rich in her total destitution? Can she really say they are her own, consider and love them as her own property, as her new self?

What do we in fact call our own? What do we look on as our self? What I can love as mine, use as I choose; what I can admire, take pride and pleasure in, find happiness and enjoyment in—in short, a centre to which I can refer everything else.

Well, the soul that has reached unitive love, having abandoned self sufficiently to merit God's invitation to the sublime exchange we have described, can really do all that with the God who gives Himself to her. She can lovingly admire His divine perfections, find an ecstasy of happiness and take pride and pleasure in them. She can henceforward perform all her actions to please God, concentrate her whole existence on Him, and really do with Him and for Him, her new possession, everything she formerly did for herself.

Yes, God is really hers. He has become as it were her new self. She can exclaim with the seraphic Saint Francis of Assisi, "Deus meus et omnia—*My* God and my all."

6. That is the unheard-of, unbelievable exchange that God's mysterious love proposes to the soul that loves Him with all her might. Be happy, soul dear to God, tremble with joy. Respexit humilitatem ancillae suae. Wretched pauper though you were, you have found favour before the great King of Kings. He has bestowed on you a loving glance and taken you into His royal palace, to raise you to the dignity of a queen. ·

Yes, henceforward you are a queen, and untold wealth is yours. Everything that belongs to God, your divine spouse, is yours. Not only do you possess the whole world with its hills and valleys, flowers and birds, the sun and the innumerable stars, but also, what is infinitely more precious, the infinite magnificent perfections of God are yours. You have exchanged your extreme poverty for the infinite wealth and majesty of the King of Kings.

So do not grieve any more, as you used to do, with glum vexation at the sight of your imperfections and personal troubles. These will disappear like a speck of mud in the ocean of divine perfections that God has given you. What does it matter to you now, that of yourself you are poor and wretched? United to God, you are infinitely rich in Him. Are not His beauty, His purity, His most pure love, all His sublime perfections yours?

7. But there is an even better reason still, simpler yet deeper, why the soul can truly say that God is hers, that all the divine perfections in which she delights belong to her.

A soul that has attained the unitive life has gradually identified herself with Jesus of whose Mystical Body she is a member. In reality Jesus lives in her. She can exclaim with the great Apostle, "Now not I, but Christ lives in me". Jesus lives in her, thinks in her, loves His Father in her. He uses her like an additional human nature wherewith to love intensely, in her and by her, His beloved Father.

With Jesus she can say to God, "*My* Father". With Jesus she considers and loves the divine beauty, divine power, divine love, divine happiness, as really her own. With Jesus she delights to lose herself in the deep abyss of the divine attributes, which are really *her* treasure, her property, her whole happiness.

One can imagine to some extent the unspeakable joy that must fill such a soul when Jesus makes her feel more perceptibly His presence and love, and when with Him she contemplates with delight the inexpressible splendour of His heavenly Father.[1]

7. Happy the souls who have attained this perfection of love, and enjoy these divine delights, a prelude to the joys of heaven. How we envy you. You have renounced paltry earthly joys, the petty joys of self, and the joys of Jesus Himself have filled you, joys as vast as the universe, as vast as God, their source and their motive.

Souls that have not yet such good fortune, strive to be more generous in forgetting yourselves. Think less of self and more of Jesus who lives in you. Above all, beg Him often, with all the strength of your soul, to fill you Himself with His most pure love. He alone must live in you. Then He will irradiate you with His own thoughts and love. He will make you see too, in some degree, His Father's lovableness, as He Himself sees it, and make you love it with His love. In union with Him, living in Him and for Him, you in turn will be able truly to say, "Deus meus et omnia—My God and my all. Yes, Father, You are *my* God, for You are the God of Jesus who lives and loves in me."

[1]We could not over-emphasize the fact that this idea is at the root of all the joys of the unitive life. The joys we pass in review in this book are joys that Jesus lives in the soul that has become identified with Him. It is really Jesus who in the soul enjoys with delight His Father's incomparable perfections. It is Jesus who by means of the soul loves His mother and sleeps happily in her arms, Jesus who in the soul delights in His divine virtues. We will return to this point as occasion requires.

6. THE JOY OF LOVING GOD INSTEAD OF LOVING SELF

1. The soul that loves self cannot find happiness in this life. The reason for this is simple, though unsuspected by many people. Happiness is being sought where it does not exist, where it cannot possibly be found, in loving self, seeking self-satisfaction, wanting to embellish this self that is the scene of so much misery and ugliness, and the source of so much disillusion and suffering.

2. To satisfy this insatiable self, the soul seeks untiringly for joy in the delights of the senses under all their forms. The soul goes around in quest of sense-pleasure—very unsatisfactory, deceptive pleasures. There is always something lacking in them. Scarcely has the soul tasted a new pleasure than the disgust engendered by satiety makes its appearance, and snatches away the brief enjoyment.

To satisfy self, the soul also tries to gratify conceit. She runs after the esteem and admiration of others. She dreams of fame. But this human glory is always very limited, often very false, and in any case the joy it causes is never unmixed.

More than anything, perhaps, the soul that loves self seeks the happiness of admiring herself, though often this is unwitting. Secretly, the soul takes pleasure in her own qualities and perfections. Then, in order to experience this joy more fully, she strives unceasingly to perfect and embellish herself.

3. Often even a generous soul, who has left the world to devote herself to the interior life, still seeks this apparently praiseworthy joy. She dreams of perfection, but a perfection which would be her own product, in which, therefore, she could find subtle self-satisfaction.

But how could this self-satisfaction ever fully content
her secret and foolish self-love? However blind a soul
may be to her own faults, she cannot but see she is full of
ills. If God's grace is at work, she soon sees herself to be
so ugly that she ends by being disgusted with herself.

Then in her own eyes she is impure, egoistic, cowardly,
vain. All these faults have an ever-renewed bitterness.
No, she does not possess, and never will possess, the
moral beauty, the purity, the nobility, in which she had
dreamt of finding some day her joy and admiration.

4. Poor soul, whichever way you turn to appease that
self of yours that thirsts for happiness, you only find
disappointment.

The misfortune of all souls that love self is to hold as
a treasure, and love as their dearest possession, something
imperfect and mean. It is a real misfortune to love as
one's own, and as a thing one would very much like to see
perfect, something that is essentially imperfect and
faulty, and that will always remain so, despite all one's
efforts. To be unceasingly forced to taste self, a draught
sweet in appearance but bitter in reality; like the unfor-
tunate moth, to turn again and again, madly, to
the flame of self that dazzles and burns—such is the
unhappy fate of a soul that loves self, that has not yet
lost self.

It must unfortunately be admitted that many souls, by
vocation consecrated to the spiritual life, never succeed
in breaking completely the many subtle bonds that im-
prison them in the bitterness of self. They never fully
abandon self, never finally enjoy the calm joy of a really
free soul that has renounced once and for all self-
satisfaction and self-love.

5. What a happy deliverance it was, soul dear to God,
when you finally succeeded, under the long influence of

a powerful grace, in becoming entirely disgusted with self, when, with a feeling of supreme contempt for the self you formerly loved so much, you finally abandoned it, threw it away like a rag, like something that didn't belong to you, renouncing self-love for ever.

Then God showed Himself to you in His incomparable lovableness. God, the plenitude of all goodness, of all beauty, of all perfection, offered Himself to you as the sole object of your love, to take the place of your wretched self, to become as it were for you a new and delightful self.

A new life then began for your heart thirsting for happiness and affection, a life filled by love. You loved more than ever now. You loved passionately and with great happiness, for you had finally found someone most worthy of your love, someone who would not disappoint your hopes. You had found the infinite and entrancing perfection of God Himself.

6. Your lot is a most enviable one, blessed soul. In place of your personal beauty, the numerous defects of which displeased you so, you now possess as your own the wonderful beauty of God, which, however little you know it, you at least know to be perfect and without the least shadow of a defect. With what pure, unmixed delight you admire it, losing yourself in the contemplation of its divine attractions!

In place of the paltry glory of this world, which attracted you and yet escaped you, you have found the vast glory of God, that is now yours, and beside which the highest human praise seems no more than a mockery to you.

In place of the wretched gross pleasures of the senses you have found the delightful and wholly spiritual joy of a soul that is plunged in the supreme and unchanging happiness of God, and shares in the limitless immensity of divine felicity.

7. You love the plenitude of all goodness, and, pitch of happiness for a loving soul, you have the intimate and incomparable satisfaction—never to be had in any merely human love—of finding your Beloved ideally lovable and perfect, of knowing with unalterable certainty that you will never find the slightest shade of imperfection in Him you love. Not only will you never love Him too much, beyond His merits, but you know you will never be able to love Him enough.

What a contrast between your present and your former life ! Merely to recall your former false delights deeply upsets you, and makes you appreciate better and more deeply enjoy the happiness that is now yours.

Formerly in your foolish illusion you loved imperfect things, you attempted without success to find pleasure in what is essentially bitter. That was your misfortune and pain.

Now you love intensely what is good and beautiful, you drink at the very source of delight, you love what is lovable in its inexhaustible plenitude, the God of all perfection. That is the purest happiness that can be had in this life of exile.

8. No doubt all generous souls do not equally enjoy from the very first the intoxicating delight of this marvellous contrast. Providing they are brave in abandoning self, however, they will sooner or later know that happiness.

When Jesus has filled them with His divine life, when they see to some extent with His eyes and love with His love the infinite perfections of God, He will grant them the ecstatic delight of a perfectly happy love, a love that has finally found in the Beloved all it had ever dreamed of, and a thousand times more.

7. MY GOD IS PERFECT IN EVERY WAY

1. There is a great happiness that is reserved only for
those who love God, never known in any human love. It
is what is felt by a loving soul at the thought that her
divine Beloved is perfect, that He fulfils all her desires
and dreams.

Whether the soul considers God in Himself, and in
His divine attributes, or in His loving care for her, she
feels the special, the unique joy of being able to say, "My
Beloved is perfect in every way".

2. No doubt the soul knows very little of what this God
whom she loves is in Himself, yet the little she knows is
sufficient fully to content her.

In the first place God's love is seen to be infinitely
superior to that of any creature. Who ever loved as her
Beloved has loved her, to the point of martyrdom on
Golgotha, to the abasement of the Host? Wonderful
manifestations of divine love, which the soul has learnt to
appreciate even better in the hours of intimacy, when
God has lovingly approached her, or made His presence
perceptible in the depth of her heart.

She has experienced a little of God's goodness in times
of trial and suffering. She has felt the caresses and consolation generously bestowed by God, whose kindness
infinitely surpasses the kindness of the most loving of
mothers.

She sees God's beauty every day under the veil of
created beauty, so splendid sometimes, in the enchanting
landscapes that fill the soul with joy, pale momentary
reflections of the eternal unchanging Beauty she loves.
Has she not more than once during such contemplation
felt herself mysteriously affected, and as it were carried
away, by the influence of that Beauty, hidden yet present?

What of the divine power of her Beloved? One need only open one's eyes. The earth, sky, sun, myriads of stars—everything hymns the power of God. What of so many other perfections of the Beloved—eternity, immensity, wisdom, immutability, happiness?

Yes, her Beloved pleases the soul. However imperfectly she knows Him, He contents her immensely, fully, completely. Besides, by her deep faith, she knows she does not know Him well, that in Himself He is a thousand times more loving, more beautiful, wiser and more powerful than she could possibly imagine. She knows He is God, that is, an unfathomable abyss of perfections and attractiveness.

How could He be other than superabundantly pleasing? What else could the soul dream of for Him? What could she wish to change in Him to make Him more perfect, more lovable? God cannot but satisfy all the desires of man's narrow and limited heart, which, even when in heaven it has become immeasurably vaster in capacity, will be completely satisfied and filled for all eternity with joy ever new, by the sight of His inexhaustible perfections.

3. The God whom she loves is pleasing to the soul, in Himself, by all His lovable perfections. He is pleasing also by His divine care for her, His loving daily guidance.

Is He not supremely desirable, inexpressibly good, incomparable Love, perfect Wisdom? The least of His wishes, His slightest desire, is for the best, is everything the soul could wish for. How could a poverty-stricken, slight, puny creature like the soul desire otherwise than He does? Could she make plans of happiness or holiness that could rival for a moment, even in the slightest detail, those of God?

Yes, she loves the dear, holy will of God, so filled with kindness, a thousand times more than her own defective

will. She loves it, and could exclaim with the Psalmist,
"Laetabor ego super eloquia tua, sicut qui invenit spolia
multa . . . Custodivit anima mea testimonia tua et
dilexit ea vehementer."[1]

A few minutes' attentive thought will suffice to make a
loving heart at least glimpse the inexhaustible reserves of
joy there are, for a soul totally given to God, in the
delightful thought that God, her love, is ideally pleasing
in every way.

4. To this great joy there is added the equally exquisite
joy of being able to tell her Beloved again and again that
He pleases her in every way, that all His divine wishes
for her please her just as His wonderful perfections do.

What an intimate, tremendous joy the loving soul finds
in telling Him she so ardently loves, that He is perfectly,
ideally pleasing to her, that He attracts and enchants her
completely. What is more delightful than to be able to
say to our Beloved that even by the farthest stretch of
imagination we could never find in Him anything to
change or improve? Married people in the world can
sometimes truthfully, and happily say, "I love you more
than anything else, you are my only treasure". But who
ever had the happiness of being able to say quite truthfully, "There is nothing I would like to change in you,
everything about you is perfectly lovable. I could not
wish you more beauty, love, wealth, power or happiness"?

Only the soul that loves God knows this intimate
happiness. With what ecstasy of love and joy in truth she
can say all that to her Beloved, that God whose beauty,
goodness, love, wisdom, power and endless felicity are
above all praise and all love. How delightful to con-
gratulate in this way the God she passionately loves, and
to pour forth loving praises, with the clear knowledge

[1] Ps. cxviii. 162, 167.

that God is the utter perfection of loveliness; that none of her praises, however high and superlative, will ever exceed the truth, will ever even be equal to it.

5. Who could describe the inexpressible colloquies of the enamoured soul with the God she loves? Sometimes it is God Himself who solicits her protestations of love, saying to her, "Is it really true that I please you perfectly? Tell Me, in what concerns you yourself, at least, would you have nothing changed in what I have chosen for you? Do you regret nothing in My past or present arrangements and desires for you?" Then the soul exclaims, in a transport of love, "Yes, Beloved, I love You perfectly, just as You are, I love Your plans for my happiness and sanctity. You love me a hundred times more and better than I love myself. How could I imagine anything better than Your divine wishes for me? Yes, I love them all ardently, I consent to them all. And if one or other of Your divine designs involves suffering for me, so much the better, how I love it! I have no other desire. You are my heaven, my all. Deus meus et omnia."

Sometimes in the exuberance of her joy the loving soul turns to the Blessed Virgin, her mother, or to her brothers and sisters, the saints in heaven. Then her joy is redoubled when she praises her Beloved and tells them, too, how much God pleases her. She knows they will perfectly understand her, she knows in advance their reply to the question she puts with touching simplicity, "What do you say of my Beloved? Are you perfectly pleased with Him too? Don't you think I am right?"

6. But this unmixed happiness is only fully enjoyed by someone who associates himself, identifies himself, with Jesus in loving in this fashion. Then this happiness, already so great, is suddenly transformed and is haloed with a reflection of the joys of heaven. For it is in the

name of Jesus and on His account, with something of *His*
joy and *His* love, that the soul, identifying herself with
Him, speaks to God and exclaims, "Infinitely lovable and
wonderful Father, You enchant me; infinitely wise and
loving Father, You please me unutterably". It is Jesus
who utters His love and overflowing joy through the lips
of the loving soul. He who contemplates to their very
depths and enjoys eternally, in the bosom of the Trinity,
the infinite perfections of His Father, now says again and
again in ecstasy, by means of the soul united to Him,
"Deus meus et omnia. My God and My all".

7. No doubt this happiness is not always equally intense,
otherwise the earth would no longer be the earth, but
heaven.

In the days of divine consolations and passive love,
especially when the soul feels Jesus' life and love irradiat-
ing her, this happiness becomes a real exaltation. Sometimes there is difficulty in controlling it. The soul would
like to proclaim aloud to everyone the perfections of her
Beloved.

More often the loving soul remains calmly under the
influence of these thoughts. They are as it were a soft
pillow on which she is asleep to the noises of the world
and forgets her own wretchedness. These thoughts fill
the hours of mental prayer and divine office, of works of
apostolate and charity. They even overflow into all the
actions of the day by ceaselessly calling forth loving
aspirations. Then suddenly this joy retreats to the very
depths of the heart, creating perfect contentment (though
this may be scarcely, or not at all, perceptible), or else
makes way, for a while, for other thoughts and other joys
of love.

Finally God often leaves the soul a prey to distressing
aridity. Then she finds herself face to face with herself,

with all her imperfections, lack of generosity, her frequent falls into self-love. Each of her innumerable ills makes her groan and suffer. God makes her taste for a time the bitter wormwood of hideous, detestable self. Then, at a moment of greatest affliction, perhaps, God suddenly snatches the soul from self, and, manifesting Himself once more, enchants her with the renewed charm of His divine loveliness. Then the soul has redoubled delight. By the striking contrast between the horror of self, and her loving God, she appreciates even more keenly the perfections of her Beloved, and exclaims more ardently, more lovingly than ever, "Yes, my God, You are truly everything I can desire, everything I could ever dream of. You please me perfectly, beyond words. You are my God and my all, for time and eternity."

8. LOST IN GOD

1. The soul that lives in faith and love gradually comes to live almost uninterruptedly in the presence of the Beloved. As she progresses in that respect, she is plunged more deeply into an abyss of unsuspected happiness, for she is now lost in God, whom she loves. Her Beloved, who loves her, is always beside her, around her. His presence fills and penetrates her. Inadequate words that hide great happiness, of a kind unknown even to the happiest of married people.

Let us even now try to understand, to catch a glimpse of this happiness, until the blessed day comes when a choice grace will make us experience it for ourselves.

2. In this life, hours of perfect intimacy are rare. Even

those who love one another most, and want to be always together, have to endure nearly every day all the kinds of separation imposed by duty and circumstances.

How much happier is a soul that really lives in union with God. She is never separated from Him. Even when she is not thinking of Him, her Beloved is thinking of her, and stays with her faithfully. The soul is conscious of this, and derives much happiness from it. Yes, loving soul, you know that the great God who is present everywhere, your Beloved, is with you always. Like the life-giving air that surrounds you, He surrounds you on every side with His unceasing care, and His love never tires of doing good.

3. He whom you love and who loves you is always near you. Better still, and this is something unique, unheard of, He is also within you. "In ipso vivimus et movemur et sumus," says the Apostle. "In Him we live, and move, and have our being." God really penetrates us through and through, forming as it were one life with ours. Ineffable mystery of divine intimacy which is chiefly brought about by the gift of sanctifying grace. It would be impossible to imagine a closer or more perfect union with one we love.

On this earth those who love live side by side yet are always in a sense separated. Even if they are sometimes brought closer to one another in a loving embrace, this does not really make their lives one.

The soul is more privileged. Immersed in God, like a sponge in the sea. At every moment He is present in the soul as well as around her, with a presence that is continually beneficent. In the fine expression of St. Augustine, God is the "soul of our soul". Happy the person who realises this fact. He lives, as one might express it, a life in common with God, a life that is as it were an unceasing embrace, a mutual loving compenetration.

A person that not only was aware of this truth by faith and savoured it by loving meditation, but also knew it by experience, mystically, wrote the following lines, moving by their very simplicity.

"In passive prayer, God takes possession of one's whole being by the power of His embrace. In these happy moments it is no longer I who am there, but He. I no longer see myself, I see only Jesus. I am not destroyed, but His life takes possession of me, dominates and absorbs me. On my knees, I no longer know myself, I see only the Son of God, really present. I adore Him, but the divine action penetrates and transforms my adoration; God thinks, lives and loves in me, and I have no life except for Him. As the Apostle said, 'Now not I, but Christ liveth in me'."[1]

4. This happiness of knowing oneself immersed in God, whom we love, is all the greater because He is both most loving and most lovable, because He is both infinite Love, and infinitely lovable.

First of all, God who loves us is infinite Love. Yes, He who surrounds us on all sides and is within us is immense, indescribable Love. Let us try to realise all the happiness this thought implies for us. Try to understand it with living and joyous comprehension.

What happiness to know oneself thus surrounded by Love itself, at the mercy, as it were, of Him who, being infinite Love, loves us intensely, unutterably. Surely the greatest misfortune on earth would be to be surrounded by one's enemies, handed over defenceless to their fury; this misfortune would be all the greater in proportion

[1] *Journal Spiritual de Lucie-Christine*, edited by Fr. A. Poulain, S.J. Cf. 14 Oct. 1887.

as their fury were more powerful, irresistible, and cruel.

In the same way the greatest happiness is to be at the disposition of God, who loves us, to be willingly, joyfully, delightfully the defenceless prey of divine love. This happiness is all the greater from the fact that God, who surrounds us and is present within us, loves us with a most ardent, and at the same time most powerful and benevolent, love, capable of making us perfectly happy.

5. To be lost in the Beloved, engulfed in Him who is Love itself! What more could I long for?

Yet my happiness is even greater and deeper, for He who always surrounds me and fills me with His presence is not only Love itself, but infinitely attractive Lovableness.

He is the infinitely perfect Being who contains in Himself all possible imaginable perfections: goodness, beauty, wisdom, power, love, purity, holiness, happiness—every good quality, charm or attraction I could wish Him to have. My Beloved has all these, to a greater extent and in a better way than I could ever imagine. I could spend my life looking for a fresh quality that He lacks, but I should never find one. He is ideally lovable.

What a happiness to think that I am thus engulfed in Him who is essentially desirable, surrounded by incomparable Goodness, under the constant regard of perfect Beauty; in short, to think of all these lovable perfections of my God, that hold me in their net, and cry out, "Beloved soul, avid of love, satisfy your need of loving, love more and more, love Me as your own. All I have is yours. Love Me with all your strength, and find all your happiness in this love. You will never love Me more than I deserve. I, who am infinitely lovable, will never fail your love and your joy, for in your love you will never exhaust My infinite lovableness. You will never love Me adequately.''

6. Such is the great and peaceful happiness enjoyed by souls united to God, souls who, in their contemplation, like lovingly to gaze at the God who surrounds them with His love and His lovableness; by souls who practise what has been called the prayer of simple regard; by souls who even in the midst of their various occupations reserve the best of themselves for God, in whom they live and who at every moment preserves them.

This happiness is even more eminently and exquisitely enjoyed by souls who identify themselves, to the best of their power, with Jesus. For it is in union with their most loving Saviour, living in them, that they lovingly contemplate God, whose tender care surrounds them. This communion with Jesus gives a special charm to their contemplation.

Moreover, Jesus loves so much to give Himself to His beloved Father in these souls and by them, and there are so few souls that permit Him this great joy, that when He finds a soul who identifies herself with Him and gives Him full liberty, He is consoled, and in compensation inundates that soul with His overflowing love that had so often been denied expression. Then He lets that soul by a heavenly light glimpse the divine perfections somewhat as He sees them. Having thus set that soul on fire with divine ardour, He gives Himself to His Father, by means of that soul, by love most pure and most happy.

9. JOY OF SURRENDERING ONESELF TO THE DIVINE PERFECTIONS

1. No doubt it is a great joy to know that we are lost in God, our Beloved, and to think of the ineffable Love and Lovableness that unceasingly surround us and attract our hearts.

Yet another joy offers itself in the thought of the loving and beloved Perfections in which we are immersed. This is the joy of surrendering completely to them and their beneficent action.

I know that around me and in me are these wonderful divine perfections, which I have long loved. Each is there with its particular charm, always active in my regard, infinitely desirous of communicating itself to me and making me feel its precious influence, infinitely desirous of uniting me to it as much as is possible. I find great happiness in surrendering, abandoning myself to them. Could I imagine anything more desirable than to be under their divine control?

2. The infinite wisdom of God, the wonderful wisdom that governs the stars of the sky and directs in perfect harmony the immense symphony of the universe, is, I know, near me, in me, lovingly watching over me, carrying out with infallible certainty His plans of holiness for me. Let us surrender joyfully to this Wisdom, to be its toy, its plaything, so that the divine plan, so wise and loving, may be carried out perfectly, without any obstacle from us.

There is the divine beauty, of which even a faint reflection has been sufficient even in this life to ravish in ecstasy so many mystics. Sometimes its mysterious charm makes itself felt in me, the better to win my heart. To it also I abandon myself with loving joy, overcome by its divine attraction. I surrender to it, begging to be entirely captivated, and detached from all finite and ephemeral beauty. I give myself up to it, so that the divine beauty may remove even the slightest stains from my soul and make it shine with a new ray of the sanctifying grace that already makes it divinely beautiful.

3. Near me I also gaze with joy on the divine purity, so dear to me. I entrust myself to this purity with a love that is in proportion to my horror of filthy earthly defilements. What a happiness, above all in time of temptation, to give myself to this Purity, who desires so much to give Himself to us, and to make us chaste and faultless as He is, and who feels infinite compassion for us when He sees us a prey to the furious attacks of the flesh.

I also entrust myself to the matchless goodness of God, who gazes at me lovingly, holding out His arms to me. At certain times God's goodness manifests to me its tenderness, greater than a mother's, and invites me to calm filial trust. How good it is, especially in days of trial, when my heart is weary or a prey to fear, to take refuge in the arms of this loving Goodness, blindly trusting in His beloved action, and peacefully sleeping there like a favourite child.

4. Divine love also encompasses me on all sides, that infinite love of which Calvary and the Host are the wonderful revelations; that living, active Love who is infinitely desirous of possessing me wholly. With what ecstasy I offer myself to Him, that He may at last drive from me the self-love that horrifies me, penetrate and set me aflame with His consuming fire.

Finally the divine felicity surrounds me too, immense ocean of peace and joy, whose waves would bathe my soul somewhat even in this life, as a foretaste of the happiness of the elect. How could I not eagerly plunge into it, losing all remembrance of my petty troubles and trivial sorrows?

Yes, all the divine perfections that I feel near me are there, and many others, ready to unite me to them, desirous to shed something of themselves upon me, before engulfing me entirely in heaven. Each of them envelops me with its own special and most blessed influence.

5. If I really love God with filial trusting love, will I not find great joy in thus submitting myself to the beloved and longed-for influence of the divine perfections? These perfections, thanks to God's grace, are no longer for me as they are for so many Christians, mere pale, cold abstractions without influence on my spiritual life. For me each of them is now a living, active reality.

In the course of my prayer, according to inclination, I can think of myself as surrounded by one or other of them, converse familiarly therewith, offer thanks for past favours, ask to be made more and more supple and docile to its influence, and open my heart fully to its divine action.

Or, if I so prefer, I can abandon myself to each of them, repeating lovingly, "Adveniat regnum tuum, fiat voluntas tua". For each desires to diffuse itself more and more, in order to rule unimpeded in me, and each has its plan for me, its designs, intentions and loving action.

Moreover, outside the time of prayer, by an ardent aspiration of my soul, by a simple thought of this or that perfection, I can renew my self-surrender. In this way I can maintain quite simply, without any din of thoughts or words, my consciousness of these lovable perfections, so prodigal of themselves, so tirelessly and mysteriously active in my soul, in order to bring it to perfect union with God, that is, to sanctity.

10. INVENI QUEM DILIGIT ANIMA MEA[1]

1. In the depth of every human heart, God, in His desire to be loved by us, has hidden an inborn, transcendental, deep-seated love that makes it secretly, profoundly enamoured of God, the perfect Good.

Our soul is hungry and athirst for God. Without perhaps being conscious of it, the soul is essentially directed, like a magnet, to God. Our understanding has being for its object and therefore seeks God, desires God, the supreme and infinite Being. This need impels it in its search for truth and is the cause of all its activity of knowing. Our will has good for its object, and desires God, the perfect Good. It is this insatiable desire that ceaselessly impels our will, supplying the motive of all its activity.

2. The human soul, therefore, by its very nature, loves God. Strange as it may seem, that is true of everybody, even of hardened sinners who avoid God, and hate Him. Unfortunately this innate, natural love of God is not known to the great majority of men. They are quite unaware of its existence. Hungry for a perfect good, they seek and think to find what they search for among earthly things, which have some element of good in them, but are a mere dim reflection of the infinitely lovable God, who is really what men long for. Men thirst for God, for perfect happiness, but do not know the pure, fresh spring that would fully satisfy their thirst. Instead they drink at the pools of salt or muddy water that creatures ceaselessly offer them, and only increase their thirst. Poor mortals, they have a need, a passion for God, but they run blindly in their unconscious pursuit of God, and everywhere find disillusion. St. Augustine had known

[1] I have found Him whom my soul loves (Cant. iii. 4).

this endless disappointment when he exclaimed, "Thou
hast made us for Thyself, Lord, and our heart will be
restless and unhappy until it rests in Thee."

3. Worldly people, therefore, are continually mistaken
in their search for what they love, perfect happiness,
where it does not exist, and never could exist, that is,
apart from God. But even among the faithful who know
God and seek their happiness in Him and in the fulfil-
ment of His most holy Will, the majority scarcely realise
the deep love and longing for union that secretly burns
in their hearts. They love God, they even love Him more
than anything else, but they do not love Him as their sole
and perfect treasure. Besides Him, they love the
creatures that surround them and offer some element of
good. They love them less than God, no doubt, yet, in a
way, in addition to God, and as it were apart from Him.
They do not think of loving God in creatures, do not see
that these things are but a very imperfect likeness of God,
that what is attractive and charming in them is in reality
a ray shining from some perfection of God Himself.

4. The soul has to devote herself in real earnest to the
spiritual life, and be really fervent before she can discover the secret passion for God that is rooted in her very
being. How many divine graces that implies! Spiritual
trials and consolations must long exercise the soul, and
much time must pass before she can become aware, with
some degree of clearness, of the love which God has im-
printed in her. Numerous and varied graces will finally
make the soul realise from personal experience that God
is truly her Beloved, the great, the sole Good for which
she longs, the perfect Good that satisfies all her desires,
however limitless they may be, and that apart from Him,
everything is sheer nothingness.

"Deus meus et omnia." At last the soul can truthfully

say, "You are my God and my all. It was for You, Lord, that my soul was made, and I did not know it! It was You I passionately loved, without realising it! It was You I was really seeking in the transitory attractions of creatures, without suspecting it."

5. Who could describe the immense and intimate joy of a soul that has found in God the object of her love? It is a joy as deep as her love itself. "Inveni quem diligit anima mea. At last I have found Him whom my soul loved," she exclaims exultantly. "I have found Him and shall not let Him go. Tenui eum nec dimittam. My love for Him will be eternal."

How could she let Him go, how could the soul ever abandon her divine Beloved? Does He not satisfy the deepest longings of her very being? What could she desire apart from Him? Without having seen Him face to face in this world, she has at least glimpsed His perfection and tasted in contemplation His ineffable sweetness, sufficiently for her to find only disgust in anything apart from Him. In comparison with His surpassing beauty, everything else seems ugly, beside His most pure love, the rest is mere egotism. Compared with His, all kindness is indifference, all wisdom ignorance, all happiness bitter melancholy.

6. You love, blessed soul, Him for whom you were created, and you are happy in your love. Your happiness will only increase as your love increases, and as your knowledge of your divine Beloved becomes more perfect. Already, perhaps, He has let you taste by experience, in the depth of your heart, that passionate love that before was hidden there unknown to you. He has, perhaps, aroused in you sentiments that you were not acquainted with, sentiments of passive love. Then you asked yourself, in your delight, the source of the heavenly light that

shone in your heart and made you love the divine perfections.   Perhaps He has even bestowed on you the
indefinable mystical sentiment of His divine presence, a
precious gift which He alone can grant. At certain times
you feel, by personal experience, that your Beloved is in
the very centre of your soul, at the apex where the very
faculties of the soul are indistinguishable. You feel that
He loves you and that you love Him with unitive love.
Sometimes you even experience in the depths of the soul
as it were an intimate spiritual embrace that fills your
whole being with an ecstasy of love. In truth you love
God deeply. Not only do you know and believe you do,
but you now feel it. You sometimes enjoy with great
delight this love you feel; at all times it gives you peace.
You have now no other desire, no other thought, than to
give free course to this passionate love, to love ever more
perfectly Him whose lovableness is beyond all love.
Amor nunquam dicit satis. Love never says, Enough.
7. My soul also, through God's liberality, has discovered,
perhaps long ago, the innate essential love that God implanted in it. You too have understood, in the light of
living faith, or even perhaps by the personal experience
of ardent love, that you also are made for God, for Him
alone, made to love Him as your only love. Thank His
infinite goodness for the great graces and indescribable
joys He gives you. You are most fortunate. You have
found God, your Beloved. That is the sum-total of the
spiritual life. Above all, give up your heart whole and
entire to love and the joy of loving. You have nothing
else to do on this earth. Love with your whole heart,
passionately love the infinitely lovable God for whom
you were created. Let Him be more and more truly and
in very deed your sole treasure. Love Him always and
everywhere. Love Him alone, but love Him even in the

innumerable creatures He has placed around you, and whose good qualities have no other purpose in the divine plan than to make you think of Him. Then everything else will fade from view. God alone, your Beloved, will fill all things, and your whole life will be an ardent, a passionate pursuit of Him.

II. JOY IN GOD'S HAPPINESS

1. If love makes us share in the good things of those we love, it above all makes us share in their most precious possession, as it were the fruit and sum of all the rest, their happiness. Parents experience themselves all the ups and downs in their children's happiness, and their children likewise share the joy of those they love more than anyone else.

Consequently it would seem that the soul that loves God truly and profoundly ought to be deeply happy, if not emotionally, at least in the will, on account of the happiness of the God she loves more than herself, more than everything else.

2. Yet, strange to relate, how many generous, loving souls seem indifferent to the divine happiness! If they are asked whether God's happiness plays a large part in their life, whether it is a habitual subject of their intimate thoughts or meditation, they will reply with some embarrassment that as a matter of fact they rarely or perhaps never think about it, and that God's happiness for them has been like something that does not exist, something that has had no influence on their lives or on their individual happiness.

What is the reason for this strange and regrettable anomaly? Partly, perhaps, a lack of living faith, but more the deplorable fact that such souls think of themselves too much, and live too much within themselves. Their love, though sincere, has not become pure enough to make them live more in God than in self, to make them share in His life and joy. In a word, their love is not yet unitive love; they do not know the joys of the life of union.

3. A generous, self-forgetful soul, on the other hand, thinks very seldom of self, except with contempt and loathing, but thinks often of God, whom she loves with all her power, and thus gradually comes to delight intensely and almost continually in the happiness of God.

No doubt this delight is not always felt emotionally. Hours when God's felicity overflows the soul, and fills it with ecstatic joy that affects the emotions, are followed by hours of calm peaceful happiness of an almost imperceptible and unemotional kind, affecting the will alone. But whether emotionally felt or not, joy and peace are present, in an increasingly habitual manner, because the soul, living more and more in God, shares more and more intimately in all His goods and perfections, especially in His happiness, and thus to some degree begins to live the life of heaven.

4. The thought of God's happiness soon becomes almost instinctive by dint of being habitual. The soul as it were breathes the divine happiness. Everything, for that matter, invites her to do so.

When she thinks of the divine perfections (and she very often does so), when she thinks of the power, wisdom, beauty and lovableness of her Beloved, and of the infinite love with which the persons of the Trinity love one another, the soul almost automatically thinks of the infinite joy these perfections give God, and this causes her an intimate satisfaction and peace.

God is infinitely perfect, she thinks. He has in Himself everything He could wish for, and possesses everything that I could wish Him. Nothing is lacking to His perfection or His happiness. What a joy it is to know that! If I had in myself everything I could wish for, it would certainly be a great happiness. But if God possesses in Himself all I could wish for Him, and a thousand times more, my happiness should be very much greater and purer, since I love God incomparably more than myself.

5. Such are the delightful sentiments which the contemplation, or even the mere remembrance, of God arouses in the soul that lives in union with Him. Even if her glance leaves God and falls on the innumerable things of this world, this only makes her thoughts return to the supreme happiness of God.

Everything speaks of her beloved Lord, His divine perfections and the joy they cause Him. She only has to open her eyes and look at nature. The vast blue sky, with its admirable arabesques of stars, speaks eloquently of the God who is not only great and powerful, but finds ineffable joy in His power and greatness. Every flower, a blade of grass, the smallest insect, proclaim unceasingly— "Be happy, for God your Beloved is great, powerful, beautiful and perfect, and His perfection gives Him infinite happiness".

6. A loving soul loves to think constantly of the happiness of her Beloved. She is joyfully lost therein, as if in a boundless sea.

Sometimes, despite her powerlessness to do so, she tries to imagine a little what the divine happiness must be. She searches her past life for memories of intense happiness. She recalls the rare moments, happiest of all,

when God's presence, most felt, made her forget all
created things and taste heavenly joys. Such moments
are most blessed and unforgettable.

At other times the soul thinks of the joy that filled
with ecstasy the hearts of the saints and made them exclaim, "Satis est, Domine—It is enough, Lord, it is too
much happiness", or which for instance wrung this
sublime cry from St. Mary Magdalen of Pazzi, "If a single
drop of what I feel in my heart were to fall into hell, hell
would at once become heaven".

Yet these heavenly delights are only a faint reflection
of God's own happiness. The soul knows this, and so,
transcending all these joys, rising higher and higher
through the "Cloud of Unknowing", like the lark intoxicated with sunlight, she is intoxicated with happiness
at the thought that everything imaginable is nothing,
absolutely nothing, compared to the infinite essential
beatitude of God, her Beloved.

6. Such communion with God's happiness is all the
more dear to a soul united to Him, in proportion as she
finds in it the expression of a purer love, and a closer
union with Jesus. She thinks of God's happiness less on
her own account, to feel its delightful effects on herself,
than for God's own sake. Her joy is in Him, not in
herself, and for that reason it is stable and lasting.
Whether she *feels* God's happiness or not is of little importance—she *knows* He is eternally, indefectibly happy.
Faith makes her sure of that, and her love is content.

Now this joy of the soul in the thought of God's happiness is in fact Jesus' joy in her. Jesus lives unhindered
in such a soul, communicating to her all His sentiments,
joy and sadness. How then could she be indifferent,
unaffected by God's felicity? Jesus prays and loves in her
and must therefore impart the exquisite joy He feels in

lovingly contemplating His Father's bliss. That infinite bliss belongs to Jesus, therefore to the soul as well. It is not surprising, therefore, that at certain times the soul is penetrated with joy, and loses herself with Jesus in the immensity of divine felicity.

The soul truly loses herself therein, finding the total forgetfulness of self for which her disinterested love thirsts, forgetfulness of her physical sufferings and mental sorrows. No doubt she loves suffering because it makes her resemble Jesus, her crucified spouse. She loves to give the Master who dwells in her the joy of being able to suffer in her and by means of her. Most often, however, her very pure love prefers to forget and transcend even suffering, prefers to forget her whole being in order to think only of the ineffable bliss enjoyed by God her Beloved.

7. To be sure, nobler and less personal sufferings often affect her. The sight of the miseries of this world saddens her. Charity makes her feel for other people's sufferings. Zeal inflicts a deep incurable wound at the thought that Love is not loved. Yet even in these holy sorrows she usually finds without effort great consolation in the remarkable joy of continually communing with the eternal happiness of God.

8. This joy is indeed remarkable, and as changeless as the changeless joy of God who is the cause of it. A joy that nothing can take away, neither her own imperfections nor the sins of others, for all these things do not affect God. God is God, infinitely happy. He is and always will be God, always perfectly happy.

This participation by unitive love in the divine felicity creates inexhaustible joy in the soul, a joy that resembles the beautiful lakes that are set like emeralds in high mountains. They are clear and still, and nothing ruffles

c

their surface. Even the storms raging around them do not disturb their peace, for they are sheltered by the glittering peaks of eternal snow. Such is the deep serene joy of a loving soul, perfect and changeless amid the storms of life, for it is protected on all sides by the dazzling summits of the divine perfections. Such a soul can always exclaim happily, "Sufficit mihi si Deus meus vivit—It is happiness enough for me to know that my beloved God is living and infinitely happy."

9. "O my God, how ashamed I am when I think how little I have thought until now of Your divine felicity. How many times I tell You of my love over and over again, calling you, with the seraphic St. Francis, 'My God and my all.' What mysterious reason has made me think so little of Your happiness, as if I hardly loved You? Why is it I scarcely ever even remember Your infinite bliss, which everything ought to call to mind?

"Alas, like too many people, I am still too wrapt up in self. My horizon is bounded by my own petty joys, trivial fears, selfish sorrows, personal worries. Perhaps I often think of Your divine perfections that concern me more personally and satisfy my self-centred spirituality, your goodness, merciful love, loving wisdom. But the perfections that concern You Yourself seem to mean nothing to me. Who will make me leave self more and more, who will help me to fly far from myself, to rest and live in You, my God? Quis dabit mihi pennas et volabo et requiescam in te, Domine? Heavenly brothers and sisters, saints who even in this life knew the joys of pure love and shared so perfectly in the divine life, obtain for me something of your love, so that forgetting the passing joys and sorrows of this life, I may finally, like you, be plunged in the ocean of divine happiness.

12. THE JOY OF LOVING ALWAYS

1. When a generous soul begins to be consumed by the flames of divine charity and has understood to some degree that her Beloved is above all love and can never be loved enough, she feels an ardent and growing desire to love unceasingly, unremittingly, always and uninterruptedly. She would like never to do anything but love, and express incessantly and in innumerable ways her love for God, who has won her heart, and thus make her whole life homage and a continual love-song.

But unfortunately the soul's desires seem very powerless. How many details in the day seem devoid of love. How many hours even, when the dear thought of Him she loves, and whom she would like always to think about, does not even enter the mind. The poor soul suffers strangely from the weakness of her love, feels its continual fluctuations very bitterly. Yet divine charity is continually growing in the soul, which gradually attains the life of intimate union with Jesus. Gradually also the consciousness of loving Jesus always increases, and with it the great joy this knowledge imparts.

2. To love always, and to do nothing else except love, such is the happy state to which her divine master has gradually led the soul. She loves, and knows now that she loves, even when she seems quite cold and indifferent. By frequently renewed assurances, and secret intimations in the depth of the soul, Jesus has made her fully realise that there are innumerable very different ways of loving, and that, whatever the state of the soul, she can always love in one way or another, in the way He has chosen for her.

3. The soul loves when, in prayer, she lovingly admires the divine perfections of her Beloved, finding in them

satisfaction, joy and pride. She loves also, as she well knows now, when, cold and arid, she suffers at not being able to fix her glance of loving admiration on God, even though a few hours before she had done so with delight. This very suffering is an effect of love, as Jesus has often shown her.

The soul loves when, in prayer, she expresses her feelings in burning words, but loves no less when, silently resting like Magdalen at the Divine Master's feet, she calmly listens to Him, loving Him peacefully, deeply.

She loves when, in prayer, she gives herself to Jesus by an explicit, affectionate gift of self. But, as she knows, she loves also in giving herself to Him many times a day by a simple heart-felt glance, without words and almost without thinking.

There is a love of the soul which unites one to God throughout the day by short repeated acts of union, as well as a love that remains united to Him by simple orientation of the will, prolonged almost unconsciously. 4. We love also by expressing affection by our various forms of activity, by the innumerable details of daily life, the kisses, caresses and flowers of small sacrifices of which St. Teresa of the Child Jesus used to speak, and by means of which we tirelessly strive to give Jesus pleasure and delight His divine heart. It doesn't matter whether this love is called self-sacrifice, unselfishness, zeal, charity or trust, whether it is consoling, joyful, emotional, or, on the contrary, anguished and painful. It is still the love of God in one form or another.

There are even very quiet, inconspicuous forms of love that the loving soul herself is scarcely aware of, at least at times. None the less they please Jesus, who shows the soul so. For example, there is the love that makes us sad at seeing the Saviour so little loved, that makes us sympathise with Him in His loneliness and keep Him company. Then there is the anguished love of a soul struggling in a violent storm of temptations and stretching out beseeching arms for help from on high. Above all, there is the desolate love of a soul passing through the furnace of passive purification. Far from feeling the joy-giving presence of her Master, she thinks she has driven Him away for ever by her infidelities and lack of generosity.

5. What needs to be stressed, for the consolation of many generous souls (though those who have attained the life of union with Jesus well understand it), is that it matters little whether our love for God is explicit, deliberate, and fully conscious, or simply a spontaneous, hidden love of which we are not fully aware. Many souls do not sufficiently realise that our hearts can form incessant acts of love, direct acts, unanalysed, not expressed, yet most precious. These acts spring uninterruptedly from a loving heart, just as minute particles are exhaled continually from flowers, and form their scent.

A mother who spends a night keeping watch by her sick child obviously does not only love it at the occasional moments when her love finds expression in actual words, loving caresses and tender kisses. She does not cease to love, even when she does not think of loving or of showing her love. Every moment imperceptible acts spring from her heart, making her vigil an uninterrupted act of love for her child.

It is just the same as regards our spiritual life. How many of our fears, sorrows, joys and hopes are motived by love of God! When we are saddened by the crimes of evil men, pleased by the fruitful apostolate of zealous

people, we are loving God without realising it, by innumerable direct, tacit but true acts of love. When we
are saddened by the long absence of God, our Beloved,
when our affection seems to have chilled, we are still
loving. Our prolonged, dumb sadness tells Jesus all the
time how much we love Him.

6. Very many loving but faint-hearted souls, lacking in
trust, would do well to assimilate these consoling truths.
They would have more alacrity, enthusiasm and holy zest
in the service of their Divine Master if they were deeply
convinced that they can love all the time, and, moreover,
that despite many imperfections and ills they really love
Jesus unceasingly and please Him from morning till night.
To know that would certainly transform their lives and
give them wings, as it changed the life of St. Teresa of
Lisieux. They would sing her love-song: "To live for
love is to give without counting, without claiming any
reward in this life. I give without counting, of course,
for love does not calculate. To the Divine Heart overflowing with love I have given everything. I travel light.
I no longer possess anything. My only wealth is to live
for love."

7. Fortunate souls, intimately united to God, who
understand these truths! Jesus has so often encouraged
you in periods of aridity and consoled you after His long
absences, that you have come to know with unshakable
certainty that nothing interrupts your love. Ceaselessly,
sometimes in an agreeable, sometimes in a dry, arid
manner, you have the great joy of loving your Beloved
always, and of knowing you love Him. Your life is
indeed splendid, overflowing with love of God, radiant
with the joy of pleasing Him. The innumerable creatures
you chance upon each day are for you so many flowers
from which like diligent bees you tirelessly gather the

honey of Divine Love. Beautiful flowers like roses—
goodness, beauty and joy, faintly suggesting perfections
of God, raising your minds to Him and inviting you to
love Him. Flowers bitter as worm-wood—opposition,
suffering, difficulties, stimulating love and eliciting self-
sacrifice. From morning till night everything is a
motive for loving, for love is all you see or look for in
everything, for you it is the very breath of life.

In order to avoid too much repetition, we have here
envisaged the soul in so far as her love is personally her
own. But a soul closely united to Jesus, identified with
Him, never looks merely at herself. She always sees herself united to Him, enriched by all His virtues, above all
by His love. She loves God unceasingly by means of the
infinite love of Jesus Himself. Her joy at loving always
is therefore really much truer and more perfect. Cf.
The Joy of Giving Jesus, p. 101, The Joy of the Communion of Saints, p. 121.

PART II. JESUS

13. DILECTUS MEUS ELECTUS EX MILLIBUS[1]

1. One often hears people speaking with sincere though rather disdainful pity of those noble and generous persons who, bravely breaking with all the pleasures and joys of the world, have (as the worldly-wise think) wasted the springtime of life by burying themselves in a cloister to consecrate themselves to God in a loveless and joyless existence.

It is a great pity, people say, never to know the best, most agreeable and most exquisite thing in life, to sacrifice the joys of love without even having known them, and stoically to repress the profound needs of the human heart which, in the springtime of life, like sap in the trees, tend to dominate our whole being.

Those who talk in this fashion do not realise their mistake. Poor worldly people, they imagine they have a monopoly of love.

They do not know that their love and joy are very little compared with what souls consecrated to God experience. They don't suspect that it is they who are pitied, that such souls regard them with a smile of deep and sincere compassion. The fact is, they have never realised the penury of the merely human compared with the supernatural ideal, the infinite nothingness of the love of creatures when compared with the love of God.

2. What is it in fact that earthly lovers love and call their treasure ? A little delicate, ephemeral beauty, the beauty of a rose that blossoms in the morning and withers by

[1] My Beloved, chosen out of thousands (Cant. v. 10).

evening, a beauty that is merely relative. Which of them
can say with justified satisfaction that the man she loves
is more handsome than any other, that the woman to
whom he has given his heart is incomparable, unequalled
in beauty?

Their treasure is a little love, ardent perhaps, delightful, but seldom pure and perfectly unselfish. In any case,
a love whose intensity will diminish from day to day, and
whose delight will gradually fade.

What they love is a little kindness, gentleness, friendship, tenderness. But even the most lovable characters
have their faults and disagreeable traits.

They love a little wealth, but jealousy makes it seem
inadequate, and a stroke of misfortune may swallow it up
from one day to the next.

They love health—but health which, despite appearances, is never proof against the unexpected, and may be
ruined for ever by unforeseen circumstances.

A little beauty, love, kindness, riches, health, for a
few short years—that is what worldly people call their
treasure, that is what they love. Perhaps they will say it
is a very great deal. Yet how little it is, how extremely
little, how ridiculously paltry for the human heart,
thirsting for the infinite, hungering for perfect and
eternal happiness.

3. How contemptible it all is compared to the pure joys
of love that you experience, soul consecrated to Jesus,
spouse of Christ, the infinitely lovable and perfect.

Jesus whom you love is ideal and perfect beauty—
beauty ever young that even in this life has rapt in ecstasy
so many saints and in heaven holds the elect in an eternal
ecstasy of love. No doubt you do not yet see face to face
that Divine Beauty, but what does that matter to a loving
soul? The chief thing is not so much for you to enjoy it

yourself, but to know by faith that it exists and that Jesus your Beloved enjoys it ineffably. Moreover, have you not sometimes, in hours of contemplation, experienced the mysterious charm of that Beauty, very slightly, perhaps, yet sufficiently to be able to say with legitimate pride, "He whom I love is more beautiful than all, and beside Him all creatures are mere ugliness"?

Jesus is also incomparable love, the undisputed prince of love. Who has ever loved as Jesus has loved you? Who, to win someone's heart, has ever done what Jesus has done to win yours? Who ever suffered, as He did, the martyrdom of the Cross, for those He loved? Jesus' love is unequalled in intensity, unequalled in purity. Beside it worldly love is mostly mere egotism, self-love in disguise. Instead of waning, Jesus' love will always become more ardent, till it becomes the ineffably happy love of heaven.

4. Jesus is also wonderfully kind. He is the inexhaustible source of all kindness, a drop of which, placed by Him in a mother's heart, produces the marvels of self-sacrifice that delight and astonish us.

He is the model of all the most winning virtues—humility, meekness, mercy, charity and the rest, which are so varied and attractive to a loving heart.

Jesus whom you love is also the infinitely rich lord and owner of all things, the glorious and powerful king whose sceptre governs every creature, in heaven, on earth and in hell, to whom the whole universe and the millions of vast worlds of which it is composed pay a ceaseless tribute of magnificent praise.

Finally, Jesus is Life—the multifarious life that vivifies all things like inexhaustible sap, giving them some share in His creative action. He is eternal Life, unchangeably identical with itself though all things pass and flow away.

Jesus, your heart's love, is all that, and not merely for a few brief years, not even during your life-time on earth only, but essentially, indefectibly, for all eternity.

5. Could one imagine a more striking contrast than that between the objects of human and divine love, between the worldly ideal and the ideal of the cloister? On one hand there is love for a very imperfect creature whose qualities fade and gradually lose their attraction; on the other there is the love of the infinitely lovable God, endowed for all eternity with all the perfections that could captivate and fill with happiness any heart capable of loving.

God's infinity and the nothingness of creatures are incommensurable. No comparison can be drawn between these two loves, or between the joy given by them. As the sky is immeasurably above the earth, so is the joy of loving the infinitely lovable God superior to that of loving a mere creature.

Soul who loves Jesus, you love the infinitely lovable, you love your God, you are the spouse of the King of Kings, the Lord of heaven and earth. Is this not enough to satisfy your love, to captivate your heart and enkindle in it the intense flame of divine charity? It is understandable that, in times of Divine visitation, in the hours when your Beloved takes you to His heart and reveals His secrets to you, manifesting something of His divine perfections, you are as it were intoxicated, beside yourself with love. Then you understand something of St. John of the Cross saying: "If you had seen a ray of the glory of my Beloved, you would endure a thousand deaths to see it again, and having seen it again, you would want to die again in order to see it once more". What earthly bride could ever say that?

6. A soul consecrated to Jesus does not envy human

love. Would a queen envy the rags of a beggar-woman,
or covet what she loves? Far from being envious, such a
soul deeply and sincerely pities worldly people. Sometimes she feels like proclaiming to them: "You think
you have found love and the true joy of loving. You have
not. You have found a mere fleeting shadow. The only
love worthy of a human heart in its entirety is the love
of Him who alone is perfectly, ideally lovable, of Him
whom we could never love too much, never love enough,
whose illimitable claims on our love will always exceed
our capacity for loving. It is love of the God who
created our heart for Him, and who alone can fully
satisfy it. If you knew Him whom I love, if you could
see what I see with the eyes of my soul and feel the love
He awakens in my heart, you would no longer feel disdainful pity for me, but irresistible, well-founded envy.
Dilectus meus electus ex millibus. My Beloved, chosen
out of thousands."

7. Yet, unfortunately, we must admit that many souls
consecrated to Jesus do not enjoy as they ought the
delight of loving Him. Their faith is not living enough,
their love not great enough. Jesus is not really the one
and only treasure of their heart. He has not become a
real spouse to them. Or else it is that they have not
glimpsed sufficiently His indescribable charm, not appreciated sufficiently in their prayer the attractiveness of
His divine perfections. Others would profit very much
by reflecting more on their greatness in Jesus, their
nobility as a spouse of Christ, and the immense good
fortune of loving Him who alone is perfectly lovable.

Happy the soul with living faith and ardent love.
Everything recalls her divine Beloved, everything sings of
His ineffable perfections, everything speaks of joy and
love. The flowers, birds, sun, stars, the whole of nature,

innumerable in its marvels, the sight of the crucifix, of
the Altar,—everything, from morning till night, pro-
claims: "Happy spouse of the Most High, privileged
creature whom the Lord Almighty has chosen for Himself out of thousands, love your Beloved with all your
might. You have nothing to do in this life except follow
the deepest need of your heart. Love your God immensely, you will never love Him as He deserves, and as
you ought."

The faithful soul is indeed most happy. Everything
around her helps her to keep clearly in mind the fact that
even now in this life she is the spouse of God. The precious and almost continual consciousness of this fills her,
as can easily be imagined, with pride, peace and joy. She
exclaims sometimes, with St. Bernard, "Nec Lingua valet
dicere, nec littera exprimere, expertus potest credere
quid sit Jesum diligere. No tongue can tell, no pen
express, only experience can teach what it is to love
Jesus."

14. QUEEN OF THE UNIVERSE

1. The soul that has chosen Jesus as her sole treasure,
and is united to Him by complete self-donation, feels
profound joy, as we have seen, at the thought of the
infinite perfections of her divine Beloved. The thought
of her union with Jesus also fills her with a legitimate
pride and dignity that raise her above the hundred and
one trivial things of this world and perfect the peace and
joy that spring from her love for Jesus.

2. Her Beloved is riches itself. What are all the jewels,
the fortunes, the possessions that the great people of this
world take pride in, compared to God's treasures? The

whole universe and all its marvels are His. What are princely houses and the gorgeous palaces of kings? Is not the whole world the incomparable palace, the magnificent temple of the Most High? The soul's Beloved is the Lord of Lords, and the proudest monarchs of this earth are but His humble vassals and owe Him incessant tribute of homage and admiration. Yet the soul, which before was only one creature among many, has become, by her alliance with Jesus, the spouse of the King of Kings, the queen of the universe.

History has known peasants and poor insignificant beggar-women whose great beauty has won the heart of a king and raised them to a throne. Such persons were fortunate, happy, universally envied. But what was their happiness and change of rank in comparison with what falls to the lot of a soul united to Jesus? What is a transitory earthly kingdom compared to the surpassing dignity of a spouse of God and queen of the universe?

3. The saints well understood the indescribable nobility and incomparable greatness of a soul raised to union with God. That is why kings have abdicated, royal princes and princesses have scorned the crown that one day was to have graced their brows, in order to give themselves to God in the poverty of the religious life. Far from thinking that they lost by this renunciation of all their possessions and glory, they rightly considered they were gaining immeasurably in dignity by it. Far from having the slightest regret at the thought of their immense sacrifices, they experienced inexpressible delight merely to recall the blessed day when they had exchanged a temporal crown for a crown of eternal glory. In their transports of joy, they exclaimed with the Apostle, "Omnia ut stercora arbitror, ut Christum lucrifaciam. I have considered all things as dung that I may gain Christ."

4. A soul that has chosen Jesus for spouse ought often to re-read that magnificent song of praise, Psalm 44.[1] The sacred singer praises both the beauty, power and splendours of the Messiah, and the noble happiness that belongs to the faithful soul, His spouse. First, he sings the praises of the King: Thou art beautiful among the sons of men: grace is poured abroad in Thy lips; therefore hath God blessed Thee for ever. Gird thy sword upon Thy thigh, O Thou most mighty. Myrrh and stacte and cassia perfume thy garments, from the ivory houses, out of which the daughters of kings have delighted Thee in Thy glory.[2]

Then, continuing the royal marriage-song, the psalmist speaks to the queen: Hearken, O daughter, and see, and incline thy ear, and forget thy people and thy father's house. And the king shall greatly desire thy beauty, for He is the Lord thy God, and Him they shall adore. And the daughters of Tyre with gifts, yea, all the rich among the people, shall entreat thy countenance.[3]

The soul that is espoused to Jesus ought often to meditate on this psalm, in order to appreciate more and more her greatness in Jesus, and to realise better her astonishing nobility. By doing so, she will protect herself all the better from the seduction of the various trivialities of this world. How could she, queen of the universe as she has become, sink to the vile, despicable things she formerly loved but which are now quite unworthy of her rank? How could she still think of sharing her affections between creatures and their Creator, between imperfect and transitory things and the great King of heaven and earth whom she loves? For indeed, what does she lack? What could she desire that she does not already possess? The whole world is now hers, in Jesus and through

[1]Vulgate. [2]Verses 3-4, 9-10. [3]11-13.

Jesus. She can say with St. Agnes, the admirable virgin
of Rome: "Ipsi sum desponsata cui angeli serviunt, cujus
pulchritudo sol et luna mirantur—I am espoused to Him
whom the angels serve, Whose beauty is the admiration
of sun and moon".

5. In truth, the soul that lives as a true spouse of Jesus
and is imbued with the sentiment of her dignity is infinitely rich, and is seldom unmindful of her wealth.
The flowerets sown at your feet by your Beloved for your
delight in their beauty and sweet odours, the birds He
sends fluttering about you to charm your ears, the
streams, forests, mountains—everything is yours. All
nature belongs to you. The whole world is the garden of
your Beloved, in which you walk, leaning on His arm,
irradiated with His love.

In your transports of overflowing joy you can truthfully apply to yourself these words that St. John of the
Cross puts in the mouth of the soul vivified by love.
"The skies are mine, and the earth, nations, the just,
and sinners. The angels are mine, the Mother of God
and all created things are mine. God Himself is mine,
and for me, since Jesus Christ is mine and for me. What
do you need to ask for or seek, then, my soul? Is not
everything yours, intended for you? Do not lower yourself. Do not linger over the crumbs that fall from the
table of your Father. Leave your low estate and glory in
your grandeur. Lose yourself therein and take pleasure
in it, and you will possess all that your heart desires."

15.   JESUS: JOY OF EARTH, JOY OF HEAVEN

1. Among the numerous titles which we can give our divine Saviour, there are few that make Him as attractive to us as that of "Joy of the world", and few that are so unaccountably forgotten. "Yet, beloved Saviour, if we love You, we only have to think of this fine title of praise, only to recall that You are the joy of the world, for our hearts to fill with intense delight.

2. "You are indeed the joy of the world, of the millions of human beings that people it. No doubt this vale of tears in which we live has many sorrows, but it has many joys too. There is not a single one of these joys that is not derived from You. You are the divine sun of joy that gives light to the world, penetrating everywhere with beneficent rays, shedding joy even in its darkest corners.

"Joys of the natural order, in endless variety. The joy of a happy mother lovingly caressing her new-born baby. The joy of a wife arm-in-arm with her husband. The joy of children playing near the parents they love. The joy of an artist gazing with profound content at a masterpiece he has at last completed. All these joys and hundreds of others come from You, Jesus, who in Your loving kindness cause them to glow and throb in hearts indifferent, ungrateful, hostile to You.

"The supernatural joys of those who love You. The intimate joy of those who in Holy Communion receive You with love in their hearts. The joy of a soul that finds You at last after long days of aridity and desolation. The joy of those privileged persons to whom You impart the exquisite mystical sentiment of your Divine Presence. The joy of the entranced soul to whom in contemplation You reveal something of Your inexpressible Beauty. All these joys come from You. You alone in your infinite goodness make them blossom in our hearts.

"How many joys You love to bestow in our lives! Ocean of felicity, you take pleasure in giving us something of your happiness. Even a few drops of that happiness are enough to make us to exclaim: 'Nec lingua valet dicere, nec littera exprimere, expertus potest credere quid sit Jesum diligere'. In truth only the soul that has had the happy experience, knows how sweet it is to love You.

3. "Jesus, You alone are the joy of the world. You are the happiness that all passionately desire. You alone could say in all truth: 'If anyone thirst, let him come to Me and drink'. Lord Jesus, we all thirst, with an immense, unquenchable thirst for happiness. If everyone knew You, if they knew that You are the pure and only fountain of all joy, that all created happiness comes from You, how souls would crowd to You and love You!

"How delightful it is for me to think that You, my Beloved, the spouse of Your poor weak creature, are the joy of this great world, the joy of the millions of men that inhabit it. What pride I feel in saying over and over again, 'Jesus, my Beloved, Joy of the World'. What happiness I feel in loving You and saying again and again, 'Most lovable Jesus, I take You to my heart, I love You, love You a thousand times for all the happiness and joy that You bestow on the world, and for which so few are grateful to You.'

4. "But, Divine Master, you appear more attractive and lovable still, and I am even more exultant, when I consider You on high as the Joy of Heaven. Joy of the Father, Mary's joy, joy of the myriads of angels, joy of innumerable saints who gaze on You, lost in an eternal ecstasy of love. I love You, Jesus, for being all that. I

bless You for the immense goodness that makes You find happiness in imparting Your bliss to all the elect throughout eternity.

"You are the joy of the Father. In You, He contemplates with delight the perfect image of Himself. In You, as in a spotless mirror, He loves eternally, and with ineffable bliss, His divine perfections. Hic est dilectus meus in quo mihi bene complacui. You are indeed His beloved Son, in whom He is well pleased.

"You are Mary's joy. Who could tell the happiness which You eternally bestow on your Mother, whom You love beyond measure? Your omnipotence and limitless love exhaust themselves, one might say, in order to make inexpressibly happy the woman who was Your incomparable Mother and overwhelmed You with her tender maternal love.

"Finally, You are also the joy of the millions of angels and saints who enjoy the unimaginable bliss of Paradise, and will spend their eternity contemplating Your divine perfections. Sun of divine happiness, Your heavenly rays only reach us in this world through thick clouds, dulled and lessened. Our very dispositions prevent You making us happier. But up among the elect You shine with all the brilliance of Your infinite splendour. Nothing intercepts the warmth of Your rays, there is no obstacle to Your loving and beneficial influence. For the blessed in heaven You are an unfathomable, incomprehensible abyss of joys ever new. Heaven, for them, is You, Your ineffable perfections seen face to face, without which heaven would no longer be heaven.

5. "Joy of the world, joy of our souls, joy of heaven— among all Your titles to our love, Jesus, there are few as fine, few as apt to win our hearts and fill them with happiness. Reveal to all loving souls the attractiveness of

this title, so little known and loved. Make them know something of the delight it implies. Grant that we may find our happiness, a happiness springing from very pure love, in thinking often of the ineffable goodness of Your Divine Heart, which takes delight in making us happy and shedding on us some drop of its heavenly bliss.''

16. JESUS' JOY

1. One of the chief needs and greatest joys of love is to please the person we love and whose love we wish to win, to be agreeable to him, cause him joy and happiness. Young married people, for example, whose love still retains all its freshness and intensity and illusions, are constantly preoccupied with, and experience a constant need of, trying to please one another. And what is the tireless pursuit of happiness, which is one of the laws governing human life, if not the perpetual desire and insatiable need of procuring for self (that object of all our affections and purpose of all our activity) an endless variety of satisfactions and delights? Pleasures of the senses, satisfaction of pride and vanity, the pleasures of art and learning, the charm of friendship, the magic of love—all these things are only a variety of means of causing some pleasure or delight to that self we passionately love. Our talents and activity, our whole life, everything, is at the service of our pleasure and joy, on account of the tireless self-love that lives and rules in us as our absolute master.

2. Now when a generous soul, under the action of grace, has begun to perceive all the horrors and ill-effects of this

self that is the object of her untiring worship, she soon
understands the immense folly of such idolatrous self-
worship. She sees that in future it will be impossible for
her to love self deliberately, for it deserves only contempt
and hatred. She soon thinks of nothing except devoting
herself entirely to Jesus, incomparable Love, supremely
lovable. Gradually the constant desire of pleasing herself
gives place to a perpetual need of pleasing Jesus, who
has become as it were another self, much dearer to her
than herself, and on whom her new activity is focussed.

To please Him and make Him happy, she gives herself
to Him fully and without reserve. To please Him, she
abandons her whole life to Him. Soon she has no other
desire, no other ideal, than to be a continual cause of joy
to Jesus. That is also why she strives to become identified
with Him, asking of life henceforward only one joy, that
of being the joy of her beloved God, and only one satisfaction, that of letting Jesus act as He pleases in her and
by her, to His complete satisfaction.

3. She hungers and thirsts to please Jesus and give Him
joy. It is the very breath of life for her to delight her
Divine Master. The whole of life appears only under that
aspect. Each single thing is valued in relation to the joy
it gives Jesus. This new passion, this preoccupation with
pleasing the Beloved, is ceaselessly nourished by the
thought that Jesus is above all love, that we can never
love Him enough, that we can never please Him as much
as we ought.

This passion soon becomes so predominant and im-
perious that the soul, endlessly seeking new means of
pleasing Jesus, ends by finding her greatest happiness in
what before caused only sadness and bitterness. What is
the desire for suffering that consumes a loving soul, if it
is not the intense, almost irresistible need of pleasing the

Saviour by every means, especially the most effective ones that imply most love of God and self-forgetfulness? 4. But real love necessarily brings joy. What then will be the joy of a soul whose whole life overflows with love and who has no other ideal or care than to please Jesus, who lives in her and by her? A fountain of happiness wells up in that soul at the thought that she can use, sacrifice, her own insignificance, and transform it into divine joy. A single smile on Christ's lips surely means more to her than the bitterest suffering, and is worth a whole life of work and sacrifice. What is her infinitesimally small life compared to God?

What a happiness it is, therefore, for a soul that ardently loves Jesus, to know that not only acts of heroic virtue, but also the smallest detail in the day, can be changed into divine joy. What happiness to be able to say that the point of her whole life is to give joy to Christ, her God. If she could choose one name of all names, it would be Jesus' Joy.

Be happy, loving soul, joy and delight of Jesus. .You well deserve your noble title, for you are a delight to Jesus, not only sometimes, but from morning till night. You please Him, the King of the whole universe. You make Jesus happy—Jesus, supreme goodness, infinite love, incomparable perfection, your royal and divine spouse. What bliss beyond compare! You pray, act, speak and suffer for no other reason than to please Him. You use eyes, ears, lips, heart, mind and will only for His satisfaction. Anything to make Him happy, to let Him use all you have have and are for His greater joy and delight.

6. No one lived on these ideas more than St. Teresa of Lisieux. Her dominant thought, her aim and object in life, was to gladden, console and please Jesus. It is the

leitmotif of this book too. Shortly before she died she
summed up as follows her life devoted to loving:

"I have always remained little, with no other occupa-
tion than gathering flowers, flowers of love·and sacrifice,
and offering them to God in order to please Him."[1]

"Great saints," she said on another occasion, "worked
for the glory of God, but I, who am only a little soul,
work only to please Him."[2]

For her the whole of the spiritual life was reduced and
simplified into one thing, the constant endeavour to
please Jesus. So it was she wrote to one of her sisters,
"If you want to be a saint, it will be quite easy. Set
yourself only one aim, to please Jesus."[3]

Happy we should be if we could imitate, even from
afar, the great saint of Lisieux, above all if we could
gradually acquire, like her, a real passionate longing to
please Jesus. Then like her we should have the happiness (though perhaps not emotionally felt) of being
able to fill our whole life with Christ's joy. Our whole
life would be like a precious chalice of joy which, by
gladdening the Sacred Heart, would make us happy too.

7. All this does not mean, however, that the soul always
experiences in an emotionally perceptible way the
delightful heavenly joy of pleasing her divine spouse.
Such a thing is impossible. The heart of a creature could
never in this life contain so much happiness. Besides,
Jesus knows too well that if the soul continually enjoyed
such bliss, there would be a risk of her becoming attached
to the joy itself, instead of being attached to Him alone. [4]

[1] *Novissima verba*, p. 125.

[2] *Souvenirs inédits*.

[3] Letter 4 to her sister Léonie.

[4] However holy and noble this joy, a soul that loves with pure
love scarcely thinks of it, so seldom does she attend to herself. What
she seeks is Jesus' own joy, not the pleasure she herself finds in being
joy to Him.

So this joy, far from being always perceptible and pleasurable, is often hidden as it were in the depth of the soul and affects only the will. Often, too, it disappears completely, when Jesus steals away from the soul and leaves her once again face to face with her own wretchedness. By the light of the divine Purity, she then sees nothing in herself but self-love in all its forms. She sees herself so vile and ugly, that it seems impossible she could ever please the Divine Beloved, who is all beauty, holiness, love. The sun of the joy of Christ, which had warmed her with its cheerful rays, is now hidden behind masses of dark clouds—desolation, aridity. Perhaps even it has sunk beneath the horizon and its last beams given place to terrifying darkness—night, the dark night of the senses or even the darker night of the spirit. The soul thinks she is a thing of horror and sorrow for Him whom she ardently loved and wanted to please.

What is the poor troubled soul to do? She must seek in Jesus' Heart all she needs. She must offer her Beloved all His own divine purity, perfect love and admirable virtues, thus pleasing Him not of herself, but with His own divine Heart. In this way she will find some peace and joy in totally forgetting herself and her ills. Then Jesus takes pity on the poor soul sick with grief. He calls her lovingly, "Surge amica mea, columba mea, formosa mea et veni—Come, beloved, My dove, most beautiful, come to Me". He takes her to His loving Heart and by His tenderness and divine presence makes her feel profoundly how much, despite everything, she pleases Him and makes Him happy. Night has gone and the brilliant sun of Christ's joy shines once more on the soul, filling her with its warm radiance of love.

8. What a noble life to love God with all one's might, and what noble delight to be Jesus' joy, the joy of one's God! Such happiness is too little known by many people.

Many souls, unfortunately, love themselves too much and Jesus too little to feel the joy that belongs only to disinterested love.   Many others, despite their very real love, experience this joy very little or not at all, because, too much wrapt up in themselves, they think too much of their own troubles and too little of Jesus' lovableness. Living too much in themselves and not enough in Him whom they love, they know very little of the varied and exquisite joys of the unitive life.

Finally, other generous and loving souls enjoy sometimes the happiness of pleasing Jesus, but could and ought to enjoy it oftener.   They need a little more confidence in their Saviour.   They constantly imagine they cannot please Him because of their poverty.   If they could only be convinced that Jesus knows how to read between the lines, to use the vigorous expression of St. Teresa of the Child Jesus, how much more cheerful and bright their lives would be, abounding in energy and zest! They would know the same beneficial blossoming out that St. Teresa of Lisieux experienced when her spiritual director reassured her and convinced her that all was well and that she was pleasing her Divine Master very much.   From that day she began to run joyfully along the road of the virtues.

The life of a soul nourished by Christ's joy is a noble one, we said.   Her death also is certainly a noble one, and much to be envied.   With what calm assurance and loving peace a soul that has lived solely to please and delight Jesus sees the longed-for approach of the hour of perfect union and eternal ecstasy of love.   Death means she will finally see face to face and be united to Him whom she has so loved by faith in this life.   It means she will go and live eternally, and in a much more perfect manner, in the joy of the Saviour.   She has spent her short earthly life making Jesus as happy as she could. In return Jesus will spend His whole eternity making her blissful with His own infinite beatitude.[1]

17. JESUS' DESIRE

1. In the last few pages we have said that a loving soul finds all her happiness in making Jesus happy, that her favourite thought is to be Jesus' delight. We could have said, to be what Jesus wishes, for it is by carrying out His wishes as ceaselessly and exactly as possible that she makes Him happy. She uses constant ingenuity in finding out what they are, and in accomplishing them as perfectly as possible in her thoughts, words, actions and sufferings. Her only wish is to have no personal wishes of her own, to work tirelessly at the complete realisation of the slightest desire of our Saviour, to become as it were the pure and faultless embodiment of His holy wishes, in short, to become purely and simply, in everything, Jesus wish, without an atom of self.

2. How indeed could a soul be anything but happy in perfectly accomplishing, fully realising, and constantly being simply and solely what Jesus wishes her to be? Is there anything better imaginable than His divine desires? She has unbounded esteem for the intentions, plans and wishes of Jesus, whether they concern herself or the whole world. The will of God, as she knows, is her beloved God Himself. Jesus' slightest wish is the ex-

[1] All these thoughts are also applicable to our relations with the Blessed Virgin. We can and should be Mary's joy also. That, too, is delightful for a soul that really loves Mary as her mother.

pression of infinite Holiness, supreme Good, pure Love.
Each of His desires is infinite goodness, immense mercy,
eternal unchanging wisdom. Nothing better or more
lovable could ever be imagined or desired. "Fiat voluntas
tua sicut in caelo et in terra—Thy will be done on earth,
as it is in heaven." That is the soul's incessant prayer and
dearest wish. She knows that God's will is heaven and
that if God's will were perfectly carried out on earth,
the earth would be transformed, completely changed into
a portico of heaven.

3. Poor mortals, who don't realise these simple but
sublime truths, short-sighted creatures, who are afraid
of what God wants and continually try to escape His
Divine Will! In their foolish egotism they prefer to His
holy and beneficent designs their strange perverse
caprices, their mean, troubled inclinations, their fickle
desires that tyrannise over them, the satisfaction of which
usually brings in its train suffering for themselves and
other people. The more they follow their own will
apart from God, the further they stray from true unmixed heavenly joy, and the nearer they approach hell.

A loving soul, on the other hand, would never
deliberately think of preferring, even for a moment, her
own wishes to those of Jesus, or of opposing her will to
His. How could she prefer her uncertain plans to those
of infinite Goodness, supreme Perfection and incomprehensible Love?   Deliberately to harbour a wish
exclusively her own, to work to achieve a plan not in
perfect harmony with those of her Saviour, would seem
to such a soul indescribable madness, something really
abominable.

4. But, it will be said, people's worth is measured by
their will. If they lose their own desires and inclinations,
their activity ceases, they lose what is most their own,

their personality in fact. They are no longer themselves. All that is very true, but that is precisely what the loving soul longs for. In a certain manner she wants no longer to be herself, but to be identified with Jesus, to cease to be a trivial creature full of ills and wickedness in order to share in His divine life. That is no loss, it is incalculable profit. So all her wishes seek union with Jesus who lives in her, to be joined as closely as possible to Him, as it were to lose herself in Him. She knows, perhaps often even by experience, that it is Jesus who lives in her by grace, and acts in her as a member of His mystical body. How many times has the soul heard His blessed voice lovingly say, "Allow Me freely to love My Father in you and by means of you. Give Me your body, mind and will, your whole being, as an additional human nature so that My life may be prolonged in yours, and so that, thanks to you, I can praise, love and serve My Beloved Father."

For nothing in the world, therefore, would the soul have personal, egotistical wishes, when she can let Jesus live and love in her. She has nothing but the desire to be nothing by herself but simply what Jesus wishes. She knows that the purpose of each action and influence of Jesus in her is to love and glorify His Father, that her whole spiritual life is as it were His incessant effort to manifest by means of her His love for His Father. The soul burns to identify herself completely with this action of Jesus in her, to allow by her loving docility His divine wishes to come to full fruition in her, in short, to be as it were a living flame of love, the flame of Jesus' love for His beloved Father.

5. To be what Jesus wishes in thought, words, actions, sufferings, to be His love for the Father—such is the incomparable happiness of a soul that truly loves and

ardently aspires to union with her Beloved. What joy
to sacrifice all her personal desires and choices!

But why speak of sacrifice? For a soul that has attained
some understanding of the ineffable excellence of the
Divine Will, and whose ideal is to be united as intimately
as possible in this life to Jesus, it is no longer either
sacrifice or suffering to ignore her own wishes. On the
contrary, it is a profound joy, though one that is not
always emotionally perceptible. Suffering does not lie,
for such a soul, in renouncing her own wishes, but rather
in still experiencing, despite herself, so many involuntary
desires, so many inclinations that are tainted with self-
love, so many sentiments that are not those of Jesus in
her. How bitterly she regrets them, how often she dis-
avows these wretched things which, for all her efforts,
she never succeeds in completely eliminating! What
would the soul not give to be freed from them!

Only those who have felt this for themselves will
understand how much suffering these more or less unconscious and involuntary desires cause the soul. They
alone know how one must call on all one's faith and love
of Jesus in order patiently to endure these troubles which
Jesus in His loving wisdom permits for ends known to
Himself alone.

18. JOY AND JESUS CRUCIFIED

1. At first sight it seems strange to associate the idea of
Christ crucified with that of joy. Yet the truth of the
connection is beyond question. For a soul that loves
God ardently and lives in union with Jesus, the sight of
the Divine Crucified is both a source of deep suffering
and of heavenly joy.

At certain times, contemplating Jesus' pain, the soul keeps Him company in His sadness and suffering. She suffers with Him in His passion, feels painfully in her own heart the sufferings of her Beloved. Above all, she participates in Jesus' great sorrow, caused by the realisation of the uselessness of His passion for so many souls who do not understand His love and obstinately refuse to love God.

But besides these hours of sad loving compassion, the sight of Jesus crucified provides hours of great joy. Then the soul fixes her entranced gaze on the incomparable love of Jesus for His Father. For it must never be forgotten that Jesus died on the Cross not only to deliver us from hell and win our hearts by the sight of His great love for us, but, first of all and above all, for His Father's sake, to accomplish His holy will, and to reveal to the saints and to mankind the infinite extent of His love for Him.

2. How sublime is Jesus dying as a victim of His love for the Father. What blissful joy the loving soul finds in contemplating Him, who reveals Himself in this as the incomparable King of Love. Compared to His infinite love, that of the most devoted and loving of earthly creatures is nothing. As the heavens are raised high above the earth, so does Jesus' love transcend all human love. That is not surprising, for Jesus dying on the Cross for love of His Father is the most beautiful and remarkable manifestation in visible human terms of the infinite eternal love that unites Jesus to His Father in the bosom of the Trinity. Even in the eyes of God Himself, Jesus offering Himself to the Father as a victim of love is the very summit of love. This love is so sublime, so splendid, that it is the delight of the blessed and holds them in an everlasting ecstasy of love.

3. This love of Jesus crucified wins the soul by its beauty and inexpressible charm, and at the same time it brings much consolation. How many times she has groaned over loving God so little, so badly. How often she has longingly desired to love Him purely and unselfishly. Yet despite all her efforts she is far from loving God as she would wish, God who is lovable beyond all love! This thought is one of the most acute pains that the loving soul endures. Sometimes it is a real purgatory on earth. Who will give the soul the intense love for which she thirsts?

It is Jesus, martyr of love for His Father, who will give it to the soul. She finds in Him more and better things than she ever dreamed of. She exclaims joyfully: "My beloved Crucified, I have found in You the love that I sought so long. How sublime You are in Your love for the Father! How You draw my heart to You! How I love You, and thank You for loving Him infinitely! I have finally found the love I lacked, the love whose very name entrances me. I have found not the mere spark I sought, but a consuming flame, an immense, infinite conflagration of love. I have found it, not in my heart or in that of any creature, but in Your Divine Heart—Love Incarnate!"[1]

Formerly, at the sight of the intense sufferings of Christ on the Cross, useless for so many souls, at the sight of her own poor selfish love, the soul exclaimed sometimes with Mary Magdalen of Pazzi, "Alas, Love is not loved, God my Beloved is not loved". Now she would rather exclaim in ecstasy, "Oh joy divine, heavenly bliss, Love is loved. God my Beloved is loved, for Jesus, God made man, loves Him with incomparable

---

[1]See our book *The Virtue of Trust*, the chapter on "Trust and Jesus Crucified"

love, a love that infinitely surpasses the love of all the angels and saints put together''.

4. Sometimes one wonders, with astonishment, how it is that God, who is perfect Love and Mercy, and desires so much the salvation of all men, chose so perverse a world, when He could have created a world in which everyone would have loved Him with ardent and disinterested love, the love of a saint. Some answer, it is a mystery. Others reply, not without reason, that God deliberately chose such a wretched world because in this way He could wonderfully manifest all His perfections, especially His merciful love, so compassionate and lenient. But the loving soul, joyfully contemplating Jesus dying as a martyr of love for His Father, finds a much finer reply, that fills her with intense joy and bliss even in this vale of tears. However strange it may seem, the present world is, in a sense, the best of worlds, the one in which God is most loved and glorified. For all the guilt and crime of this world are in fact like a mere speck of mud lost in the vast sea of the most pure and holy love of Jesus for His Father. Thanks to Jesus' superabundant reparation, thanks to His infinite love, our world, wretched as it is, is nevertheless the best in the eyes of God and gives Him incalculably more glory and love than a world in which all men would have loved God like seraphim but in which the Word made flesh, Jesus the Redeemer, would have found no place.

D

19. JESUS—THE HOST

1. The Sacred Host—Jesus—has just entered my breast, bringing His infinite treasures. What joy to think that I possess within me and take to my heart all the beauty, wisdom, goodness, love, holiness and happiness there is in heaven and on earth. What is there in heaven or on earth that I could wish for, that I do not possess in possessing Jesus?

2. Jesus is within me with all His most pure and holy love. How could I not be filled with joy?

So often my soul lamented the paucity of its meagre love tainted with selfishness, and longed to love God its Beloved, somewhat as He deserves, intensely, passionately. Yet despite incessant efforts, I loved Him so little. Here at last is the immense, inexpressible love I dreamt of, most holy, perfect, free from all admixture of self. It is within me. I can take Him to my heart, for I possess Jesus, Love itself.

Let me lose myself in this ocean of love, which is mine and meant entirely for me, as if I were the only person who loved Him. Let me admire at length, in silence, the wonderful love of Jesus for His Father and for all men, and enjoy this incomparable love that is now mine. Let me find in Him my satisfaction and delight, and cleanse away in Him all the stains of my self-love. Let me throw into the blazing furnace of this divine love my poor cold stony heart, that loves so little but which, lost in the flames of the furnace, will no longer be distinguishable therefrom.

Lose also in Jesus, your infinite treasure of love, the sorrow caused by the vast egotism of the world. In the midst of the dark night that covers this world, rendered so frightful by all its sins, impurity, pride, jealousy, hatred (all different forms of the one manifold love of self), Jesus shines in you like a radiant sun of pure love. Blessed and beneficent sun that pierces the wretched darkness of this world, and brings, above all in hours of divine visitation, the radiant brightness of His pure love!

3. Jesus is also within me with all His purity, His spotless and admirable chastity. How good it is to think of that, after the temptations that assail me, sometimes so painfully, after the sadness I feel at my lack of generosity and perfection in my resistance to them. I can forget my wretchedness and happily rejoice in the perfect, spotless purity which Jesus brings with Him.

I shall never perfectly comprehend the infinite charm of that infinite chastity that delights the angels and of which a few drops sufficed to create the immaculate heart of Mary and the incomparable virgins Cecilia, Agnes, Lucy and so many others. To think that all that purity is mine!

How I love and bless Jesus' radiant purity, that is now mine, how tenderly I love this Purity that is the source of all created purity. Into its unfathomable depths I throw the world, that huge abscess of impurity, with its innumerable nameless varieties of heart-rending guilt. It will be lost therein like a few splashes of mud in the waves of the sea.

4. Jesus is within me also with all His infinite bliss, which He gives me, inviting me lovingly to share it.

Let us try to form some idea of the heavenly joy that unceasingly wells up in the soul of my Divine Beloved. Perhaps in the past I have sometimes, in hours of much spiritual consolation, felt intense happiness and exquisite peace, like a fore-taste of the joys of heaven. Multiply such happiness a hundred, a thousand, times more than one can imagine, it is still nothing compared to the bliss that fills Jesus' soul.

Or I can think of the joy that ravished the souls of certain mystics, such as Angela of Foligno, Teresa, Veronica Giuliani. Incapable of enduring such happiness, they fell into ecstasy, broke out into loving exclamations or uttered ardent words to ease somewhat their intense consuming ardour. The poor phial of a human heart was too small and fragile to contain the immensity of heavenly joy. Yet in the midst of these indescribable joys then exclaimed, "All that is nothing at all, not a drop compared to the ocean of bliss enjoyed in heaven".

"What must be Your own happiness, my Jesus, seeing that the saints are so happy. You are indeed infinitely happy, happy beyond anything I could ever imagine. Each of Your divine perfections, Your Beauty, Wisdom, Holiness, Love, Mercy, Power, is for You an object of loving contemplation that overflows into inexpressible joy. The love You have for the Father, and His love for You flood You with exquisite, indescribable happiness that will be our admiration and bliss for all eternity. Like the Father, You are infinitely perfect, and this fills You with infinite joy. How I love to think of that delightful truth, and enjoy it at leisure. What more do I need to make me perfectly happy too, as far as one can be in this life? You, my treasure, my only good, who are all I want to love in this world, are and always will be perfect, and perfectly happy. Isn't that supreme joy for me? What more could I dream of? Surely my desire for happiness is fulfilled in a wonderful manner. Your divine felicity is like a sea of joy stretching out endlessly before my eyes, an ocean of peace in which I can lose myself, and engulf for ever my petty sorrows and private woes.

5.   "Jesus, divine prisoner of our tabernacles, prisoner

in our poor hearts, it is for me that You are in the Sacred
Host, to share Your divine perfections and happiness with
me. You give me there your infinite, most perfect love,
for it to be my delight, and the destruction of my self-
love. You grant me Your entrancing Purity for me to
love it as my own good and to wash away all my
wretchedness. You bring me Your infinite bliss so that,
forgetting myself and my troubles, and all the sorrows of
this world, I may find all my happiness in Yours and thus
enjoy on earth some foretaste of Your heavenly joys.

"But to enjoy Your divine perfections more, I should
have to love more, to rise above self, transcend my
egotism, and love with ardent unitive love, live more in
You than in myself. Alas, dear Master, of myself I am
very helpless. Help me. Assist powerfully with choice
graces, so that I too may sometimes experience something of what the saints felt before the tabernacle, or
when they took You to their hearts in Holy Communion."

20. THE JOY OF GIVING JESUS

1. One of the great joys of love is to give—to give what
one has to the person we love, above all to give what one
is, to give oneself. This seems essential to love.

The interior soul knows this joy better than anyone
else. Has she not given the Divine Master all she had,
leaving all things for His sake, offering them all to Him
as a love-sacrifice, in order to love nothing but Him any
more in the world? Above all, she has abandoned herself
to Him and still gives herself each day. Her whole life
is nothing but a gift to Jesus. Each thought, word, wish

and action is an expression of love and a giving of herself to the Saviour.

Yet what is all that compared to the immensity of the soul's desires? What has she given Jesus? What is the soul herself? An abject, wretched, trivial creature, quite unworthy of divine regard. Moreover, even the love by which she unceasingly gives herself to God, however ardent it may seem, is nothing to what God deserves, or to what the soul would like to devote to Him. Her desire to love and to give herself seems boundless, so that even if she had all the love in the world to give, her needs would scarcely be satisfied.

2. If, however, we are intimately united to Jesus and closely identified with Him, we have other gifts we can make Him, more precious than ourselves and our inadequate love. We possess Jesus Himself, with His wonderful perfections and all His divine riches. His beauty, goodness, love, purity and holiness belong to us. Long ago He gave them to us, saying, "Omnia mea tua sunt— All that is mine is yours." We can therefore offer the Father the most precious of all gifts, a unique, incomparable gift, the only one He values, His Beloved Son, in whom He is well pleased.

We can make Him this oblation, infinite in value, as often as we like. A simple heartfelt glance or loving aspiration to God suffices. There are also the innumerable Masses that at every hour of the day throughout the world perpetuate the sacrifice of Calvary. In mind and will we can participate in them.

3. There is, however, yet another way of giving Jesus, which is well known to souls united to their Saviour, and makes their whole life a perpetual giving of Christ. For what is the life of such souls if it is not Jesus, the continuation on earth of His Life? Their life is to give

themselves wholly to Him, so that He may live fully and freely in them, and thus in and through them love His Father, and prolong and perpetuate His Life, Passion and Redemption.

For Jesus did not wish only to love His Father in times past, on earth, up to the drama of Calvary. His unbounded love desired much more. He still wants to love the Father in millions of hearts and lives, by means of us, by means of each of the members of His mystical body.

We are for Him as it were an additional human nature. As on earth He used His sacred humanity to love His Father to the last, so also He uses our human natures to continue to love Him, to give Himself to Him till the end of the world.

He uses our eyes, lips, mind, heart, all our being, to express His love for the Father and offer Himself to Him. Each of our thoughts, joys and sorrows is, as it were, a gift of Jesus, and a manifestation of His love, all the more splendid, the more perfect our union with Jesus, and the greater our docility to His action.

4. What delight and confidence to think that we are as it were a love-song addressed by Jesus to the Father, ceaselessly expressing His affection for Him; to think that the Father views us solely in His Beloved Son, filled by His presence, transparent and irradiated with His divine perfections.

Above all in hours of divine illumination, when Jesus makes us feel a little of the ardent love with which He loves in us His Father, this joy becomes truly exquisite and irradiates us with tranquillity and peace. How sublime and overflowing with love our life seems then! What a magnificent existence, to be giving God, every moment, even when we are not thinking about it, the wonderful gift of Jesus and His infinite love, beside

which the earth is but vile dust. Surely our dream of
great love has come true, far beyond our remotest
imagination?

5. Thus merely by remaining in union with Jesus we can
give Him to God all day long. In the same manner we
can give Him to Mary.

Our divine Master invites us to the sublime happiness
of giving Jesus to Mary by being Jesus for her. Christ's
love for the Blessed Virgin is also an inexhaustible, never-
satisfied love. Jesus' thirty-three years on earth were not
sufficient for Him adequately to express His love and
make Mary happy. He wishes infinitely to multiply His
love, by making her also loved by millions of hearts till
the end of the world.

That is why He asks of me my heart and my life, to
perpetuate His love for His Mother. He wants to entrust
His love to souls identified with Him and engulf them
in the waves of His divine affection for Mary.

6. How great my happiness if I am among those
privileged souls, who by perfect self-surrender and great
docility allow Jesus full liberty to express His love by
means of them. My part is to give the Redeemer my
mind, will, heart, my whole life, that He may irradiate
me with His filial love for Mary, and use me to make her
happy, renewing for her the intimate joys of Nazareth.
I am most happy and fortunate, for He still wishes, as
when He was a child, to express over and over again His
love for His Mother—but by my mouth now. In His
name and for Him, I can speak lovingly to her, tenderly
embrace her. In time of prayer, above all, He still desires,
through me, happily to admire her, contemplate her surpassing virtues, and tell her, "Tota pulchra es Maria et
macula originalis non est in te—You are most beautiful,
Mary, and there is no stain in you." He invites me to take

her to my heart and pour out all my foolish, loving phrases. He still wishes to make her indescribably happy, and make her re-live the pleasure she once had when she received His childish marks of affection.

It is surely unspeakable bliss, envied even by the Seraphim in heaven, to be able to give Jesus to Mary, to be Jesus for her, a mark of His love for His Mother.

7. We can give Jesus to the Father, we can give Him to Mary. We can also give Him to souls.

Jesus thirsts to give Himself to souls in every way, as He did when He walked in Galilee and Judaea. No doubt He gives Himself to us every day in the Eucharist, if we wish it, but He desires more than that. He wants, by means of all who allow Him to live in them, above all by those closely identified with Him, to give Himself also to mankind, doing good on earth, making them feel His merciful love, His tireless devotion to them, as He did during His mortal life on earth.

We give Jesus to our neighbour when He uses our lips to say gentle, kind, forgiving words, when we lend Him our hands to care for the sick and heal their ills, or our feet to seek out poor sinners whom He loves so much. Every time we practise one of the innumerable forms of Christian charity, which are the honour and glory of the Christian religion, we are giving Him to others.[1]

8. Our Saviour desires above all to give Himself to souls that they may know and love Him. He wants by means of our manifold, many-sided apostolate to win the hearts of all men for His Father. He loves to repeat through us the sublime teaching by which He detached souls from earthly things and taught them to know the real source of a happy life.

[1] Cf. Newman's fine book, *Christ in the Church.*

What is a priest if not Jesus calling little children and teaching them the secrets of eternal life, Jesus feeding the multitudes with His Flesh and His Blood, Jesus inviting the crowds to listen to the Beatitudes, telling them, "If any man thirst, let him come to Me, and drink".

What is a Sister of Charity, for example, if not Jesus, the good Samaritan, still bandaging the wounds of the sick, pouring in oil and wine, and applying at the same time to the wounds of their souls the beneficial remedy of love and repentance?

What is a missionary, if not Jesus, the tireless Good Shepherd, indefatigably seeking the lost sheep, bringing them back to the fold, that there may be one fold and one shepherd?

9. Do we who devote our lives to souls reflect often enough that we act for Jesus' sake and in His place, that it is He who is endeavouring, through our instrumentality, to make Himself known and loved, and that it is He whom we are leading to souls? Do we try sufficiently to imitate His loving-kindness, His gentleness, His self-sacrificing devotion, so that souls see Jesus when they see us? Is our ideal of being Christ to others really the ideal of each day and hour?

If we thought of that more frequently we would surely be more gay and cheerful amid the endless troubles, sufferings and weariness of our apostolate. For what greater consolation could we have than that of knowing we bring souls not a mere material advantage or solace in their suffering, but the gift of gifts, what all men long for, the Gift of God. We thus give Jesus the supreme joy of being able to give Himself to souls and ensure their eternal salvation.

10. To give Jesus to the Father, to Mary and to souls—three great and precious joys of the soul living the unitive

life. They may, perhaps, be rarely felt emotionally, for they may be hidden in the depths of the heart in the form of tranquillity and peace. Yet they are always consoling, and stimulate a more ardent and purer love.

A soul that fully appreciated these great truths described as follows the joy that she felt. "I feel more and more that my whole vocation consists in giving . . . giving God to God and to souls. That for me is perfect happiness, giving Him wholly, and always. My lot is splendid, no greater happiness could be imagined. It would be impossible for me to be happier than I am.

"At the beginning of the spiritual life, love tortures us because we love, yet cannot find a gift adequate to our love. But when Christ has united us fully to Himself, and we can, through His abiding presence, give the Infinite to God and to souls, the torment ceases. We give Him all He can receive, we do for souls everything that could possibly be done for them, and love of God and our neighbour is fully satisfied.

"Then we have only to be grateful, and give, remaining hidden in love in order to radiate it. It is delightful to give . . ., to feel there is absolutely nothing for oneself, that everything is for God and for others."[1]

[1]Cf. letter 54 in *Marie de la Trinité. Lettres de "Consummata" à Une Carmélite.* Carmel d'Avignon, 1930. Cf. also the admirable letter 32.

PART III. MARY AND THE SAINTS

1. A loving soul often experiences a pain of love un-known to the mediocre. It is the intimate sorrow, like a wound in the heart, caused by the impossibility of loving God as she would like to, and as He deserves. This pain begins the day when, by special grace, the soul first glimpses the infinite lovableness of God and of Jesus, and it never ceases to grow as love increases.

It is the pain of those rare moments of ardour in which the flame of divine love reveals more clearly the divine perfections and burns the soul in its devouring fire. The pain also of the more frequent hours when divine love seems only to smoulder in the soul, which feels cold, dry, indifferent, devoid of love, though the memory of divine perfections, however faint it may be, pursues and frets the soul very painfully, with tireless persistence.

Such sorrows are unknown to souls who do not love God with deep and tender love, and who have never really grasped that God alone should be loved, and every-thing else loved only in Him.

2. What must the loving soul do in her sufferings, where find the remedy that will cure or at least soothe her wounds ?

Far from finding consolation, if she looks around her she only sees new reasons for greater sorrow. She loves but slightly and imperfectly, but around her are souls who do not even love God at all and profane their love by bestowing it on vile, imperfect created things. The world appears a vast chaos, in which egotism rules un-disputed and unchains the basest passions. Everything is loved, except Him who alone ought to be loved for Himself, God, who by His very essence is love and lovableness. Thus the loving soul exclaims sadly with the great saint of Pazzi—"Alas, Love is not known, Love is not loved, my Beloved God is not loved".

3. Take comfort, however, generous and loving soul. Amid the cold bleak fog of melancholy that envelops you at certain times like a shroud, raise your eyes to your Mother Mary, the Blessed Virgin, Mother of fair love, Mater pulchrae dilectionis. Think of her heart, brilliant sun of most intense, most pure and holy love, and soon your sorrow will evaporate under these warm rays. You will find in Mary the love you have so dreamt of for yourself, and striven for in vain with incessant effort. In your heavenly Mother you find the love you would wish to see around you and which you strive with difficulty to evoke by your unceasing apostolate. Mary loved so faithfully, ardently, and unselfishly that her love was perfect even in the sight of God Himself. All the base and nauseating egotism of the world is effaced by Mary's great love, masterpiece of divine omnipotence and of Christ's grace.

Moreover, this indescribable love becomes yours, provided you love your heavenly Mother with unitive love. Her love is everlasting, it has never ceased or lessened in force or ardour. On the contrary, it is confirmed everlastingly in heaven, even greater than it was on earth, wonderfully intensified by the splendid revelation of the divine perfections of her divine Son, her infinitely loving and lovable God.

4. What joy to know this, to be able to gaze at Mary, to admire her and exclaim with rapture, "I have finally found the love for which I thirsted, for which I was sick with desire. I have found it, a thousand times greater and

more intense than I should ever have dared to hope, in the heart of Mary, the Mother of Fair Love. What happiness and consolation wells up in me at this thought, giving me a foretaste of the joys of heaven.''

Thus the loving soul finds great joy when she considers Mary's love for God, the joy of at last seeing her God loved with a love worthy of Him. This joy, already great, and springing from the soul's love of God, is increased by another joy that springs from her love for Mary, the joy of seeing that it is not a stranger, but Mary, our beloved Mother, who thus loves God with a love most pleasing to Him and beatifying for her. The soul had dreamt of the joy of loving God herself. Now she tastes the much more exquisite delight of seeing that Mary her Mother, whom she loves much more than herself, loves God with inexpressible love, and is filled with inconceivable joy.

5. For the loving soul her love for Mary and the joy it causes is a delightful reality, much more real and tangible than the concrete material realities of daily life. No doubt such consolation is not always equally vivid, indeed it is perhaps only rarely that it floods the soul with emotionally perceptible joy. Yet it is there for all that, always real in the depth of a soul that has meditated these exquisite truths and well assimilated them in hours of prayer and contemplation.

6. If you are sad, generous soul, because you love God so little, because you see Him so little loved, and because you have little power to make Him loved, do not forget Mary, your great consolation in these sufferings of love. Perhaps you have thought too little of Mary, the Mother of Fair Love. Perhaps you have never even thought of raising your mind to consider her perfect love of God. In the future do not forget this pure spiritual consolation

that Mary offers you. In the storm of sadness that sometimes buffets you at seeing God so little loved, do not
forget to gaze at the shining beacon, Mary, your loving
Mother.

Often tell her, tenderly and confidently, "Mary, I
should like so much to love Jesus with a great and very
pure love, but I am powerless. Love Him for me. Tell
Him of my love again and again. Manifest your love for
Him, on my behalf as well as your own, in that motherly
way which Jesus loves so much and which causes Him
heavenly joy."

Lose yourself in this way in Mary, forget self, your
miseries and those of the whole world. Share her life a
little, and her love, and thus experience in her arms, on
her breast, the joy of her incomparable love. At certain
times, at least, you will thus enjoy something of the joys
of heaven. At the same time your love for your heavenly
Mother will marvellously increase by this precious
contact with her

22. MARY, A JOY TO JESUS

1. One of the greatest joys a loving soul can have in this
life is, we have seen, the happiness of being a joy and
delight to Jesus. To delight the sole object of our love,
to please and make happy the divine Beloved, such is the
constant desire, the very breath of life as it were, of a
soul that loves Jesus with ardent unitive love.

In times of divine consolation the soul abounds in joy,
is enraptured at the thought that she is pleasing Jesus a
great deal, or even perfectly, that she is making Him
happy by each of her actions, thoughts and sentiments.

Her whole life, it seems, has no other motive than to please the Saviour, to give Him constant satisfaction. But there are other hours, of aridity, desolation, spiritual numbness, when the poor soul suffers from the idea that she is not pleasing Jesus, that she cannot please Him and make Him happy, because of all the imperfections and faults she is ceaselessly committing. A few short hours before she resembled a rose in bloom, now she is dry and withered. She reasons with herself, but in vain. She tries to convince herself she still loves, if not with an emotional and pleasurable love, at least with deeply real love. What is the soul to do? Where can she seek the consolation and delight she needs?

2. Soul dear to God, seek refuge with Mary. Forget all your ills, forget yourself. Gaze with love on Mary, your heavenly Mother, who is without any doubt at all a joy to Jesus. If you love Mary with unitive love, your tears will soon be dried, and your sadness turned into great joy.

Mary is a perfect joy to Jesus. Ave gratia plena. The Archangel Gabriel himself found her full of grace. Mary in fact is the masterpiece of Jesus' power and loving-kindness. He made His mother Mary so beautiful, pure, immaculate, holy, loving and perfect in all the virtues, that even He, infinite Sanctity and Purity, could never find in her the slightest fault or stain. She is so entrancingly attractive that even He, infinite Beauty, could say in all truth, "Tota pulchra es, Maria, et macula non est in te—You are perfectly beautiful, Mary, there is no stain in you."

3. We shall never understand in this life the heavenly, divine joy that Jesus finds in regarding His masterpiece, His wonderful Mother. Jesus is inexpressibly happy at seeing all Mary's perfections.

He is chiefly happy to see and make her happier than

all other creatures. "Beatam me dicent omnes genera-
tiones"—All generations in fact have proclaimed her
blessed. It is surely Jesus' chief delight to be able to
make His Mother, whom He loves perfectly, incomparably happy, and to contemplate the vast abyss of
happiness which His love bestows on her. Mary is indeed
in the fullest sense a joy to Jesus.

4. What happiness for me, then, if I love Jesus and Mary
with unitive love, to contemplate, at length, calmly and
lovingly, Mary, Jesus' joy and delight. What bliss to
have near me Mary, who is a perfect cause of joy to Jesus.
For Jesus' happiness is what all my desires seek, and
what caused me sorrow before, because I could not procure it. I have in Mary as it were Jesus' joy in person,
visible and tangible. What happiness to be able to love
Mary, my heavenly Mother, to repeat endless loving say-
ings to her, "Mary, perfect joy and delight of Jesus, I
love you with all my heart and soul". How could I fail
to be filled with joy? I desired so much to see Jesus
happy, to be able to give Him some little joy. Now I
have found His perfect and entrancing joy, an abyss of
joy for Him. It is like a prelude to heaven.

It would be a good thing, especially on Mary's feast-
days, to spend a good deal of time in this way in our
Mother's company, gazing lovingly at her, admiring her,
reflecting on the joy she gives Jesus. Let us, at such
blessed moments, ask Jesus who lives in us to give us
something of His mind and heart to see and admire Mary
somewhat as He sees her, and love her with His love.

23. IN MARY'S ARMS

1. We all learnt in childhood that the Blessed Virgin is our Mother, and that as well as our earthly mother we have one in heaven too, whose love for us is greater than that of any mother. So it is that in our prayers and hymns we call Mary, not only our queen or Jesus' Mother, but also our Mother.

Yet very few souls, even fervent ones, fully appreciate this truth. Very lively faith and ardent love are needed to realise that Mary is not only the Mother of all mankind, the Mother of all of us in general, but a real Mother to each of us in particular, loving us with personal love, as though she had nobody else but us to love in the whole world. In the mind of the majority of Christians, Mary is not their Mother in any practical way. For them she is not really a Mother. They do not live like true children of their Mother Mary.

2. The soul that is fully aware that the Blessed Virgin is her Mother, really lives as her child. She is not content merely to pray to her several times a day, or even to think of her occasionally outside of prayer-time. She does much more. She does what all children do with their mother, talks to Mary with loving familiarity. Even when she says little, she lives under Mary's maternal eye, conscious of her dear presence, and really spending the day with her.

The day of a real child of Mary is a day devoted to, filled and preoccupied with, Mary.

Like a little child resting on its mother's breast, she likes spiritually to put her arms round Mary and press her to her heart, to show her love and say loving things. She tells Mary her sorrows and childish troubles as well as her joys and good news. She consults her in her slightest uncertainties.

When temptation assails her, she runs like a child to take refuge with her. If she has committed a fault, she throws herself in Mary's arms and, tenderly embracing her, asks forgiveness with loving trust. If she wants to undertake some task, she asks Mary's help and blessing on her poor efforts.

Sometimes she is much affected at the thought that she has never seen this loving Mother who is much dearer to her than her earthly mother. Tears fall from her eyes in secret and she sighs for the most blessed day when she will finally be able to see her heavenly Mother and press her to her heart. Perhaps even with childish presumption she tells Mary this sorrow and asks her to show herself to her if only once, as she did to Aloysius Gonzaga, Stanislas, Alphonsus Rodriguez, Gemma Galgani and so many others.

For such a soul Mary is really a mother in the full sense of the term, a mother full of solicitude, so near and present that it is only necessary as it were to stretch out one's arms to be able to press her to one's heart.

3. Happy the soul that spends her life like this in the company of Mary, her beloved Mother, that can at all times raise her eyes to Mary and speak to her in loving aspirations. Happy, above all, because she can do everything for Mary, to please her. It is a great joy to think that the slightest thought, or effort, the least and apparently indifferent actions are all means of showing love for Mary and making her happy. The day is filled with love for Mary, and also with loving, filial joy.[1]

4. We will not however attain this state of being Mary's children, closely united to her, in one or two years,

---

[1] It must not be forgotten that during long periods of aridity, above all during the Dark Nights of the soul, this union with Mary, like the rest, seems to diminish and almost disappear. The soul then has great difficulty in living in the presence of her beloved heavenly Mother.

above all, not by our own efforts and devices. Only our
heavenly Mother can obtain this grace for us. It is no
use our merely meditating frequently on her claims to
our love, assimilating the thought that she is our Mother,
and that we must live as her children. That would not
avail much without Mary's help. She herself must, by
a special grace, come as it were within our reach, come
down to us, make us feel sometimes in a more perceptible
way her motherly love and powerful affection. Only
then will we gradually realise that Mary is our Mother,
active as a mother, surrounding us constantly with a
mother's love. Then we will begin to live almost
instinctively in her presence, like her real children.

5. Mary will sooner or later obtain for us in some degree
this life of union with her, provided we ardently desire
it and ask for it with confidence, provided also we love
her generously, devotedly, unselfishly. She is even more
anxious to obtain this grace for us than we are to
receive it.

   It is a precious grace, which will transform our life,
and fill it. Then we will look back and it will seem as if
until then we had no mother, that the Blessed Virgin
was not yet a real Mother to us, nor we her children,
that we were like poor orphans. At last, however, we
shall have found our Mother, delightful, most loving,
and her constant companionship will fill our lives with
happiness.

                    *   *   *   *

6. The soul to whom the Blessed Virgin by grace has
shown herself a Mother and who lives always in her sweet
presence as her child, will soon find her love for Mary
greatly increase. A day will come when Jesus will show
in the depths of the soul, by a very special and intimate

sentiment, that this love for her heavenly Mother that sometimes consumes the soul and makes her long for the eternal union of heaven, is not merely the soul's love, but His. It is in fact He, living more fully in the soul and penetrating her powers, who is infusing His filial love for Mary.

As the soul realises, Jesus is now asking for her mind, will, heart and whole life, to continue, in the soul and by her means, to love His divine Mother. He desires to use the soul to love Mary still on earth and prolong as it were His life in Nazareth. Such an invitation must inevitably enrapture a soul closely united to Jesus. To be of service to Jesus so that He can love Mary, to provide Him as it were with an additional heart with which to love His Blessed Mother—what more wonderful could be imagined in this life?

7. Therefore the soul surrenders entirely to Jesus' increasing love, the filial love that He felt for Mary in Nazareth and which He desires to re-live, in and by means of the soul.

As a child Jesus kissed His Blessed Mother when He woke. The soul each morning throws herself into Mary's arms and kisses her on Jesus' behalf. Mary is pleased with such filial affection, and returns love for love.

In times of prayer, above all, Jesus re-lives the joys He knew in Nazareth. Rocked in His Mother's arms, He gazed enraptured at her, and, childlike, caressed her joyously. By the soul closely identified with Him, Jesus continues lovingly to contemplate His Mother, heavenly in her beauty, masterpiece of His divine omnipotence. He admires attentively and happily her wonderful perfections and glorious privileges and utters loving praises: "Tota pulchra es, Maria, et macula non est in te—You are entirely beautiful, Mary, and even My divine eyes cannot find the slightest hint of imperfection in you."

During working hours, all day long, the soul loves Mary in Jesus' name, accomplishing every action under her motherly eyes, knowing that Mary is near, never taking her eyes away from her, knowing that everything done in Jesus' name pleases Mary and makes her happy.
8. Jesus in fact does not only want to love Mary by means of the soul, He wants to please and delight her by devoted filial love. He wants to renew for Mary the blessed hours of intimacy that made her so happy in Nazareth.

It is surely the pitch of happiness to serve Jesus in order to please His Mother, to be a source of happiness for her from morning to night in Jesus' name and on His behalf. The soul therefore submits wholely to the Redeemer so that He may make use of her as He pleases, love in her and thanks to her, and thus make His Holy Mother as happy as He wishes to.
9. It is scarcely necessary to add that Jesus is delighted to find a soul who allows Him to love Mary as He desires, a soul in whom He can express His love for His Mother. So few give Him this joy. At certain times, then, Jesus makes the soul feel how pleased He is to make use of her. He makes her understand that the exquisite joy she sometimes feels in her love for Mary is in reality the effect of His own divine joy. Mary too is enchanted at having so to speak found the Child Jesus again, in the soul, and at receiving from her the loving caresses of her Divine Son, at feeling once again the joy of His love. Each thought and word of the soul appears to her as an expression of Jesus' own love, and each action is for Mary eloquent of Jesus and a mark of His affection.

Mary also sometimes makes the soul feel how dear she

is to her. Though the joy the soul receives is usually entirely spiritual, hidden in her very depths, sometimes it becomes very intense and overflows into the emotions, becoming perceptible and pleasurable. Mary is lovingly taking the soul to her motherly heart and loving her like Jesus Himself, who lives in her.

*   *   *   *

10. It has rightly been remarked that the life of confident self-surrender is the summit of the spiritual life, and that spiritual childhood is its very peak.[1]

This blessed life of trusting self-surrender is the lot of the soul who is closely united to Jesus, and loves Mary in His Name, on His behalf, living like a true child of Mary. This life of trust is admirable in its humility, simplicity, tranquillity, peace.

11. The soul that is Mary's child accepts everything with a smile of content, having no preferences. To her the Will of God and Mary is everything, whether this will implies joy or sadness, pleasure or pain, health or sickness, success or failure, spiritual consolations or aridity. Whatever it is, it is always the dear, lovable will of her Mother that feeds and sustains the soul, just as a baby lives on its mother's milk. A delightful unalterable peace penetrates the soul, undisturbed by care or anxiety, despite innumerable troubles and perhaps very absorbing occupations. The soul is much too little to be anxious. Little children do not worry about anything, they live from day to day. They don't imagine they have to provide for all eventualities, see to what may be lacking, think of the future. That is their parents' business. In the same way, the soul that has achieved spiritual childhood confides in her blessed Mother for everything.

[1] Cf. Mgr. Gay—*Trust.*

She has little anxiety even about the holiest things which duty requires her to attend to strictly, or even about her spiritual progress. Where is she on the ladder of perfection? Has she nearly reached the sanctity to which all her desires tend? What does it matter? The soul knows that Mary is lovingly watching over her, over everything that concerns her, over her spiritual life, over her apostolate, and that the wisest thing to do is to rely on Mary's vigilant love.

12. No fear affects her any more. A child without its mother is frightened by the slightest things, timid and fearful, but when it can rest on its mother's breast it is not afraid. Mary's children are the same. In the arms of their Mother they are safe, she is the all-powerful Queen of heaven and earth.

No longer is the peace of the soul troubled by a multiplicity of ever-changing desires. A child possesses everything when it has its mother. The external world, of which it knows little anyway, matters nothing to it. Its whole life and ambition is to rest on its mother's lap, lovingly caress her, and feed at her breast. Similarly, Mary's children know only one desire and delight, to love God and their Mother, to live by her and for her. What importance, then, have the innumerable things of this world, to which they have long since said farewell? After God, Mary is their all. Everything else is nothing to them and has no attraction.

13. Happy the soul, and very enviable, who has been led by the love of Jesus and Mary to this sublime life of spiritual childhood. May we too die to all things and become as simple as children. May we too by generous love and filial trust obtain from Mary's merciful goodness the grace of one day living as her child the holy, loving, happy life of self-surrender and spiritual childhood.

24. THE JOY OF THE COMMUNION OF SAINTS

1. There are few dogmas as salutary and consoling as that of the Communion of Saints. Unfortunately the majority of Christians have little idea of the wonderful beauty and great joy that it implies. They only know what we might call its external aspect, its more visible and tangible aspect.

They know that all the members of the mystical body, the Church, are united to Jesus their Head, and through Him are united to each other. They know that the saints in heaven are in contact with us, are interested in us and pray for us, and that we in turn can speak to them, beg them to intercede for us. We can also help the poor souls in purgatory by our prayers and merits. Our dead are, therefore, not entirely dead to us. They are still living, and we can help them, tell them of our affection, be happy at the thought that they are in heaven.

These are all truths we firmly believe and which are the source of much joy and consolation, unknown unfortunately to non-Catholics.

2. Yet all that is only the exterior aspect of the Communion of Saints, as it were the body of the dogma. Its soul and inner, hidden and wonderful meaning is not even guessed at by most people. That is why the very expressive words "Communion of Saints" suggest so little to them and arouse no enthusiasm.

The soul of the Communion of Saints is the perfect, universal, disinterested charity which links all the saints to one another and ought to link all the members of Christ's mystical body and establish between them close union, perfect solidarity, full community of possessions and joys. Everything that belongs to the rest belongs in a way to us too, and, if we are loving and unselfish, is a source of very pure joy.

All the possessions and treasures of Jesus, Head of the mystical body, of Mary and the saints, of the souls in purgatory, of the Christians of the whole world are ours, belong to us. Jesus' infinite love, His ineffable loveliness, Mary's incomparable love, immaculate purity and magnificent perfections, the love and virtues of millions of saints who are true brothers and sisters to us and with whom we form an immense family, the love of so many holy and heroic souls here on earth—all that belongs to us!

To understand that well, to realise it with some vividness, is a very precious grace that we cannot too often ask of God. But it also presupposes a very great and disinterested love. Only souls that forget themselves and flee the narrow prison of their own egotism are largehearted enough, loving enough, to grasp these truths and taste the joy that springs from them.

3. Let us try to raise ourselves a little for a few moments above our petty individual interests, in order to understand how the infinite treasures of the Communion of Saints, above all how their love and all their virtues are ours, constituting an incalculable treasure for us.

First of all, if I understand the word "mine" in the egotistical sense, as something personal to me, something of which I am the author, which I can attribute to myself with secret self-satisfaction as deriving from me or belonging exclusively to me, then it is clear that the love and perfections of Jesus and the saints are not mine.

But let us reject these wretched words "mine" and "me" with the egotism that we are trying to transcend, this self which is the true and only cause of our poverty and makes us bitterly taste our indigence, our lack of virtue and love.

Let us understand by the word "mine" all that in one way or another belongs to me and constitutes a good, a treasure, for me.

In what sense then can I say that all the love and virtues of Jesus and the saints are mine and belong to me?

A little reflection is sufficient to show that the pure love which binds me in affection to the virtues of Jesus and the saints gives them to me in a certain fashion. By loving them with all my heart, blessing and approving of them, willing them as far as in me lies, finding my joy in them, sharing in them, I in a way take possession of them and make them my treasure.

A comparison will make this idea clearer. Imagine a rogue who took delight in all the crimes he heard of and said, "I'm delighted at all these crimes, blasphemies, demonstrations of impiety and atheism. I wish I had committed them myself. I should like to have sacked and robbed all the churches and driven God from every sanctuary and every mind." Such sentiments, such sharing in the sins of others, would surely reveal great hatred of God and involve great guilt.

It is precisely the same as regards our sharing in the good that others do, the affection with which we love their virtues, their holy undertakings, their success in the service of God. By loving them, by entertaining many favourable desires concerning them, we share in them very meritoriously, and all the more truly as our love is greater and our participation closer.

It would be very good to give ourselves often to these holy practices of love, to spend our meditation admiring and above all ardently loving the love and virtues of Jesus, Mary and our favourite saints, finding in their love a compensation for our poverty. Such exercises of unitive love would make us, especially in times of divine consolation, experience holy and delightful joys and at the same time would make our love more intense and unselfish.

4. I can also understand more exactly by the term "mine" what gives me delight, what I can joyfully admire, what I can take pleasure and pride in—in a word, what I can enjoy as I please. Such things are mine in the best sense of the word.

Viewed in this way also, all the love of Jesus and the saints, their perfections and virtues, their happiness and glory, are mine, provided of course I have in my heart at least a spark of that unitive love that draws us out of ourselves and makes us live in the person we love. If I love with this unitive love, Jesus in Himself and in His saints, with all their wealth and happiness, belong to me and become a source of exquisite joy to me.

I can admire the indescribable beauty of Jesus, His holiness, purity, love, bliss. I can admire them as much as I wish, knowing I shall never admire them as much as they deserve. The gaze of my intellect will never exhaust such a wealth of perfections and loveliness. I can praise them, bless them, find glory and happiness in them as if they were mine. I can enjoy them to the extent of my capacity. Similarly as regards the exquisite beauty of Mary, my heavenly Mother, her unparalleled virtues, her holy and disinterested love. All those things are mine, to contemplate at my leisure, to admire with ardent, exclusive love. They can be my happiness and help me to forget my personal hardships, sufferings and inadequacies.

In the same way all the saints, and especially those who for one reason or another are more dear to me, share their treasures and virtues with me. The ardent love of the seraphic saint of Assisi, of Angela of Foligno, of Mary

Magdalen of Pazzi is mine, and can be my joy and delight if I so wish. The burning zeal of Dominic, Ignatius and Francis Xavier and their conquest of innumerable souls are mine, and can fill my meditation and appease my thirst for souls. The virginal purity of Agnes and Cecilia satisfies my need of purity and consoles me in my painful consciousness of my wretchedness. The charming spiritual childhood of Teresa of Lisieux, her blind and conquering trust are also mine, and I can lose therein my lack of confidence, my worries and my too-human anxiety.

Indescribable limitless wealth extends out of sight before my dazzled eyes, and fills me with intense pure happiness provided I forget self, and love and participate in the good things of others.

5. But the truest and most profound reason why all the good things and all the love of the saints are mine is my close, mystical and very real union with Jesus and by Him with all the members of His mystical body.

All these members are, as it were, part of Jesus, who lives in them as He does in me, and loves in them and by them His Heavenly Father. The saints of past ages, the saints of the present day, as well as the multitude of souls in which divine love merely smoulders, all are Jesus'. They are mine too, for the Divine Master long ago gave me all that is His. He holds all His treasures in common with me.

United to Jesus as I am, identified with Him, I possess all His love. Not only the infinite love with which in the bosom of the Trinity He loves the Father and the Holy Ghost, but also the love He bestows on the whole universe, in heaven and on earth, and the love by which He loves in Mary and in the legions of saints in heaven as well as in the innumerable souls on earth who are united to Him by sanctifying grace.   This immense infinite radiance of Jesus' love is mine.   Mine also are the wonderful virtues that this love has caused to blossom in so many saints of the past and in so many heroic souls of the present day.   All these things belong to me and I can look upon them as mine and, provided I love with disinterested unitive love, I can find joy and glory therein.

6.   What a delight to think of these wonderful truths.   I used to lament my lack of love and say to Jesus, "When will You finally give me the great love that will satisfy my desires a little as well as Yours?"   Now all at once my wishes are fulfilled, more than fulfilled, in a most excellent way.   I possess a love that far surpasses my dreams.   It is as if, like a poor beggar-woman, I had asked for a few pence at a royal gate, and suddenly received all the wealth of the king himself.   He has taken me into his palace, made me his spouse, given me all his possessions!

All the treasures of the love of Jesus in Himself and in the saints are mine.   Can I not then truly exclaim, like the little saint of Lisieux, "I have finally found the love I dreamt of so much.   I wanted, if possible, to love like the martyrs and give my blood for Jesus, love like the virgins and offer Him the lily of purest charity, love like the confessors and travel the world in pursuit of souls.   Now all that has in fact been given to me.   All the splendid virtues of the saints are mine, I possess their burning love, their deep humility, their blind trust, their limitless charity.   All their virtues, all their love and their hearts burning with the flame of divine charity are mine."

How could we not be filled with joy at seeing our infinite wealth of love?   It is a real prelude to the blessed life of heaven, where in a more perfect way all good things and joys are the common property of the elect.

Our happiness in heaven will not be egotistical happiness. It will not be the pleasure of gazing at our own perfections, our own beauty and our own glory. It will be an immense happiness made up, above all, of the happiness of all the saints. We shall be much happier on account of the bliss and perfections of Mary, Joseph and so many great saints than about our own.

It would be well to think often of our life in heaven, to imagine something of what our thoughts will be, what we will love, and to try to understand what will be the cause and centre of our happiness. In this way we can begin to prepare even in this life for the life of eternity. We would share more in the joys, perfections and glory of the saints of heaven and earth. Instead of endlessly groaning egotistically about our destitution and perpetual wretchedness, we would rise above our poor petty self. We would take holy joy in the immense riches which we have acquired, by an unselfish love as wide as the very universe, in union with Jesus and by Him with all His mystical members.

PART IV. THE VIRTUES

25. "CHRISTO CONFIXUS SUM CRUCI"

It is one of the sublimest triumphs and greatest glories of Christian piety and divine love to make sweet what is bitter, to make us desire what our nature abhors, to cause splendid roses of purest joy to blossom among the thorns of suffering.

No doubt merely human love also sweetens suffering. St. Augustine's remark applies even to unbelievers: "Ubi amatur, non laboratur, et si laboratur, labor ipse amatur. When there is love there is no labour, or if there is labour, it is a labour of love." But divine love extends even further. Not only does it sweeten suffering and make it loved, but it makes it so loved that it turns to joy. The little saint of Lisieux used to say, "I have come to the point where I can no longer suffer, because all suffering has become a delight to me".

A soul inflamed with divine love not only accepts suffering with resignation and love, but ardently desires it. If she had the choice between suffering and not suffering, she would choose to suffer. That is what is called the folly of the Cross. It is in a way the reversal of our natural instinct and seems folly to worldly people. Only those who are imbued with divine love understand it perfectly.

The attitude of St. Catherine of Siena is very characteristic of this Christian generosity from which the folly of the Cross springs. Our Saviour appeared one day to Catherine and showed her two crowns, one of roses, the other of thorns, saying: "My spouse, choose the crown that pleases you best". Filled with the desire to suffer

E

for Jesus and to resemble Him more closely, she at once
chose the crown of thorns and pressed it on her brow.

This action well symbolises the sentiments, in marked
opposition to natural instinct, which are felt in a greater
or lesser degree by all souls that have arrived at close
union with the Redeemer.

2. Let us try to understand a little more clearly the
thoughts that animate souls closely identified with Jesus,
the souls of the saints, and that so strongly impel them to
love the Cross and to find their happiness in it. For it is
a good thing to meditate from time to time on the
reasons for loving the Cross instead of fleeing from it, if
we too wish some day to achieve perfect union with
Jesus, and feel the joyous, entirely supernatural love of
suffering which that union presupposes.

One motive for loving, seeking, and finding our happiness in the Cross is the compelling need the loving
soul experiences of participating in the sufferings of
Christ in His Passion and Crucifixion, the need of keeping
Him company, consoling Him, comforting Him in His
pain. In all ages generous souls have found happiness in
meditating lovingly on the sufferings of the divine
Crucified. They have been moved to compassion at the
excess of His torments. But they have understood that
true compassion cannot consist merely in pitying the
Saviour, or in consoling Him by sterile emotions. They
have wished to have compassion in a more real sense, by
sharing His pain, by assuming themselves some share in
His sufferings.

The soul that is the spouse of Christ Crucified would be
ashamed to be brimming over with joy and consolations
when she contemplates her Beloved given over to
atrocious sufferings and bitter sadness. She burns with
desire to comfort Jesus by helping Him like the

Cyrenaean to carry His Cross. It seems to her that what she herself suffers is subtracted from the sufferings of Christ, her Beloved. Such a thought naturally inflames the soul with longing for the Cross. What happiness to think that she, a poor, weak, created being, can contribute to lessen the pain of the infinite God. That is what has led so many ardent souls to those holy follies and austerities most repugnant to natural instinct.

Blessed Henry Suso, that passionate lover of the Cross, exclaimed in his transports of loving compassion: "O God, close our eyes to everything but You on the Cross, shut our ears to all worldly futilities, so that, freed from the domination of the senses, we may have no taste for anything but tears and suffering". At night, in solitude, while his brethren were asleep, he used to re-enact the tragedy of the Passion, carrying on his shoulders a heavy cross in the garden and cloisters.

St. Rose of Lima also, in order the better to resemble the beloved Crucified, scourged her delicate body till it bled, tied an iron nail-studded band round her head, bore a painful cross on her torn shoulders, spent the night fixed by two nails to a cross, uniting her prayers and sufferings to those of the dying Christ.

St. John of the Cross also used to re-enact the Scourging at the Pillar, obliging those under his authority to buffet him in the refectory, and cover him with taunts and insults.

Nearer to our time there is the famous Irish ascetic, the Jesuit William Doyle. Imitating Suso, Margaret Mary, Jeanne de Chantal and others, he cut the name of Jesus on his breast and burnt it in with iron. He made a vow under pain of sin never to avoid suffering.

3. The soul that contemplates the Passion of our Saviour knows only too well that Jesus suffered torments on the

Cross because of her, not only for her benefit. That
awakens another sentiment which penetrates a valiant
soul and gives a thirst for suffering, sometimes for terrifying sufferings. This sentiment is the need for reparation,
reparation at any price for past sins. To make up by the
folly of the Cross for the folly of abominable deeds. To
wash away in blood, in one's heart's blood as well as the
blood of the body, the sins that were the cause of so
much divine suffering.

It is true that the whole of life serves the soul as a
means of reparation, yet to the ardent eyes of love
nothing is as valuable for expiation as suffering cheerfully
endured for Jesus' sake. The soul appeals for such
suffering, wills it in all its forms: sufferings imposed by
God or the daily course of duty, as well as sufferings of
her own choice. Enmity, insults, calumny, ingratitude,
failures, as well as frightful penances, painful illnesses,
cruel desolation—everything is acceptable, everything
serves to quench the burning thirst to make reparation
for the past.

Perhaps in her innocence the soul has very little to
expiate. Nevertheless this little seems much to a loving
soul. Besides, she has not only to expiate her own
personal faults, she would like to make reparation for the
innumerable, indescribable sins of the whole world. The
soul would like to resemble the consoling angel of the
agony in the garden, and offer Jesus the soothing drink of
loving and endless reparation.

This need of reparation has always been felt by valiant
souls, but never as strongly as it has been since the
revelations made by the Sacred Heart to Margaret Mary,
those urgent requests for reparation that impelled the
saint to truly heroic penances. In the present corrupt and
sinful age, this spirit has magnificently shown itself, so

that we may say that "where sin abounded, grace did more abound" (Rom. v. 20). This unending need for reparation has been well understood in our time, and has created the congregations of souls dedicated as victims to make reparation. The whole life of these admirable societies rises before the Crucified like a sublime, immense act of reparation.

4. As well as the need to share the sufferings of Jesus in order to lighten them, and in order to make reparation, the loving soul also feels the passionate desire to show her love for Jesus by suffering, as Jesus showed His love in the Passion.

The soul is consumed by the urgent need of giving her Saviour love for love, suffering for suffering, life for life even, if possible. She knows that all expressions of her love for Christ, however generous they may be, would be incomplete if she did not give Him the best of all tokens of her love, suffering joyfully borne for Him. She would even choose, if possible, the supreme token, of which Jesus Himself spoke, when He said: "There is no greater love than to give one's life for one's friends". She would like to sacrifice her life for Him as He sacrificed His for her.

Even that seems insufficient. The soul would like to have a thousand lives in order to give them all for Christ. What is the soul's petty, trivial, unworthy life in comparison with the infinite worth of the life that Jesus, her God, gave for her? Hence the burning desires of martyrdom so frequently found in loving souls.

When St. Andrew saw the Cross prepared for him, he exclaimed: "O bona crux. O blessed cross, so long desired, so ardently loved, give me back to my Master, so that by you He may receive me, who redeemed me by you". St. Ignatius of Antioch, on his way to martyrdom, wrote to the Romans, "I beg the wild beasts that await me to devour me straightway. If they hesitate, as they did with some martyrs, I will urge them on to devour me. Forgive me, children, if I speak this way, but I know what is best for me."

5. The Cross in all its forms is an excellent means of showing Jesus our love. Consequently it is also a precious means of making Him happy.

What more does a loving soul need to make her desire and love the crosses great and small that form the very texture of this life? To make Jesus happy is the dream and ideal of her life, all she wants in the world. What do the various pleasures of this world matter to her, or the esteem and praise of others? What do even spiritual consolations matter, the holy and exquisite joys Jesus sometimes sends, if they are not a means of loving Him more ardently, pleasing Him more perfectly, causing Him happiness. In truth the soul's only joy here below is to be a joy to Jesus.

No doubt the soul knows very well she can please her Divine Master by the thousand and one details of her love-filled days. All her thoughts, desires, actions, her slightest joys as well as the least of her sufferings, are like so many sweet-smelling flowers she eagerly culls for a gift to her divine Beloved. Yet the soul has an instinctive preference for sufferings, for they seem to demand more love, and appear to be more adequate expressions of love for Christ Crucified. Moreover, in suffering the soul is sure of not falling into the temptation of self-complacency, of seeking her own pleasure, for unfortunately that happens only too easily in times of consolation and spiritual joy.

6. By the very fact that suffering gives us continual excellent opportunities to show Jesus our love, it is also for

an ardent soul a welcome means of quenching somewhat her thirst for loving.

The thirst for loving burns a generous soul but is only known to those who have caught a glimpse of God's infinite loveliness and the ugliness of self. Such souls are fortunate. The divine loveliness and divine love have wounded them painfully yet delightfully, incurably, and they suffer at not loving enough. They have one idea only, that of always loving God more, a little more as He deserves to be loved.

Souls wounded by divine love have a thirst for loving. This thirst is quite naturally a thirst for suffering. They eagerly desire suffering, it soothes their love-sickness, as do the crosses that give them so many opportunities to give themselves to Jesus, to forget self for His sake, to sacrifice themselves with Him.

This is what the great saint of Avila said, on whom an angel inflicted a wound of love. "It seems to me that suffering is the only reason for existence. It is what I ask most insistently of God. I sometimes tell Him from the depth of my heart, 'Lord, either death or suffering. I ask nothing else'."

St. Mary Magdalen of Pazzi, burning with the same ardent love, expressed her thirst for the cross in an even more sublime manner: "Not death, more and more suffering".

Margaret Mary, similarly consumed with desire for suffering, shows clearly the connection between suffering and love. "My divine Master," she said, "put in my heart such a great desire to love Him and to suffer that I had no rest from my preoccupation how to love Him by crucifying self." Elsewhere she exclaimed, "Without the cross and the Blessed Sacrament, I could live no longer".

7. In conclusion we will give, among very many others,

one very strong motive a loving soul has for finding happiness in the Cross. The Cross is the supreme means of being united more and more closely to the Beloved.

The ideal of every generous soul is to be united every day more closely, more entirely to Jesus to whom she has given herself without reserve, and who lives in her. "Oportet illum crescere, me autem minui. He must increase, I must decrease." The ultimate aim to which all the thoughts, actions and efforts of her life are directed is to die to that horrible self of whose ugliness she has formed an idea, in order that Jesus may infuse His life in her. It is to be nothing, that He may be everything in her.

What can kill self more effectively than suffering, self which is the only real obstacle to the fullness of Jesus' life in the soul, self which is so clinging, so difficult to get rid of? The soul realises this, by frequent and salutary experience. If the cross is painful, it is precisely because it detaches her from self, separates her from the trifles to which self is inordinately attached. "Mihi vivere Christus est et mori lucrum (Phil. i. 21). To die to self a little more each day at the price of whatever suffering, to leave full scope to Christ is, indeed, gain and happiness.

The form under which the cross presents itself has no importance for a generous soul, whether it be light or heavy, physical or mental, sickness, calumny, poverty, absence of the Beloved, aridity, desolation, the purifying and painful mystic Nights of the senses and the spirit. They are all welcome and give joy, for she recognises in every cross the hand of the great Surgeon who is striving to cure her of egotism and purifying her love. She sees in all suffering a message from her Beloved, who wishes to unite the soul more closely to Him.

8.   A loving soul has, therefore, innumerable reasons for loving the Cross, despite its thorns and austere, repulsive

appearance, innumerable reasons for finding joy and delight in it.[1]

However, we must not imagine that this cheerful love of the Cross is mainly the fruit of meditation and thought. It is not. No doubt the soul loves to meditate on suffering and draw encouragement from the thought of the benefits it brings. Above all, she loves to gaze at Jesus in His Passion, sympathise with the Saviour in His agony, promise Him love for love. Yet however fruitful such meditations may be, they will never produce joyful love of the Cross if Jesus does not Himself fill the soul.

For the soul to appreciate the joy of the Cross, Jesus must live in her in place of self and egotism, and infuse His own love of suffering, of which His whole life was a magnificent example. Hoc sentite in vobis quod in Christo Jesu. The soul in fact must have for suffering, not the sentiments of the old Adam, but those of Jesus living in her.

9. Consequently we must not be surprised if we are perhaps still far from feeling the joy of the Cross that we admire in souls perfectly united to God, in the saints. Such joy presupposes death to self and the full and unfettered life of Jesus in us, and is not the work of a few months or years. It demands slow and persevering work, calling for much effort. Above all, it implies repeated and prolonged intervention of divine grace, and the infinitely precious gifts of the Holy Ghost, without which nobody achieves sanctity.

The saint of Lisieux said on this subject, "Until the age of fourteen, I practised virtue without feeling any

---

[1]The Cross is also a powerful instrument in the apostolate and brings many blessings. St. Teresa of Lisieux was correct in saying that it is much more by suffering than by brilliant sermons that Jesus wants to strengthen His rule in souls.

pleasure in it. I desired suffering, but had no thought of finding joy in it. That grace was given me later" (*Advice and Memories*).

10. Above all, it must not be forgotten that joy in the Cross is not always emotionally perceptible, far from it. No doubt in hours of divine consolation we feel delightful peace, perhaps, or even very intense joy at suffering for love of Jesus, to console Him, prove our love or be more closely united to Him. At such times even less advanced souls sometimes know the joy of suffering. But most often joy in the Cross is not emotional at all. It is entirely spiritual and hidden in the depth of the soul. Only souls already closely united to their Divine Master habitually experience it amid aridity and desolation. The reason is that such joy presupposes very pure love and the full development of Jesus' life in us.

26. LOVE'S BEGGAR

1. Once a soul has made some progress in the interior life, she soon feels within her the birth and growth of a real thirst for loving. For she has glimpsed the immensity of divine love that has condescended to her in the Incarnation and loved her even to the folly of the Cross. She has sometimes realised in her prayer the loveliness of God, a faint ray of which is sufficient to inflame her with raptures of love. God has been seen to be alone infinitely lovable. The soul could never love Him enough, or in any way even remotely worthy of Him.

Then the cry of Jesus in agony on the Cross rings in her ears unceasingly. "Sitio—I thirst." The Saviour thirsts for love. He begs for love. He burns with desire to receive the homage of our hearts. The soul realises that the thirst continually increasing in her, preoccupying her more and more, is essentially the thirst of Jesus Himself living and active within her.

The only aim and object of her life henceforward is to love more and more, to love to the pitch of folly the lovable and loving Saviour. Yet even that is so little. She would like not merely to love with her own heart, but also with the thousands of hearts that Jesus invites but who remain deaf to His call. She would like to fill these hearts with love and bring them to the feet of Jesus, the King of Love.

Mother Marie-Madeleine Ponnet expressed in these ardent terms the thirst for love that consumed her. "My thirst for God to be loved is becoming a burning thirst. O my God, I am like a being that is nothing but thirst, insatiable thirst for one thing only—to love without limits and perfectly to accomplish Your good pleasure, and to make it loved and accomplished. I feel that everything else is as empty as nothingness and cold as death. O my God, I thirst for You, I am dying of thirst. Give me to drink, give my brethren to drink. I thirst on behalf of souls who have not this thirst. I want satisfaction for myself and for them. I should like to die engulfed in You, overcome by excess of You."[1]

What can the soul do, in her insatiable desire, to satisfy her endless need of love and making others love?

She will make herself a beggar for love. The very idea delights the soul. Others can avidly pursue wealth and honours, enjoy the bitter and deceptive pleasures of the senses. She has in mind one thing only, to go collecting

[1] *Vie de la Mère Marie-Madeleine Ponnet*, 6e édition, Paris, Téqui, p. 274.

the alms of love, from morning till night, in order to console Jesus, make Him happy, love Him and make Him loved, as far as in her lies.

3. How can the soul beg for love, and where?

First of all, around her, by devoting herself tirelessly to others, winning hearts in all kinds of ways in order to win them then for Jesus. To say a kind word is to beg for love, so is to dry the tears of the suffering, or to give good advice, encouragement, help of one sort or another, or to soften embittered hearts by a forgiving word.

Begging for love means also to make others see the divine perfections that have fascinated the soul herself. It means making Jesus attractive to others, teaching them how much the Saviour has loved them, how much He thirsts for their happiness as well as their love.

Above all, begging for love signifies praying to the Father of all light and grace, asking Him urgently to take pity on His poor creatures, to save them at all costs, by giving them if necessary those powerful graces that the human will is not likely to resist. Prayer is the supreme means of begging for love, mental prayer, and even more the incessant uninterrupted prayer of ardent desires, united to suffering and sacrifice.

4. For in fact a loving soul wants to beg for love not only near and around her, but throughout the world. She would be willing, if necessary, to run, as so many others have done, to the ends of the earth in order to save souls, ready to endure the burning sun of the Tropics or the ice of the Poles. Even that would seem little. She would like to be in every country in the world simultaneously, begging for the hearts of Indians, Negroes, Esquimaux, as well as those of the unbelievers and atheists of Europe. Has she not an interest in the hearts of these millions of men? They too must be inflamed with divine love. How

can that be done if not by prayer? Only prayer united to suffering can multiply her apostolate indefinitely and conquer multitudes of souls for Jesus.

St. Francis Xavier knew this well when, exhausted by difficult journeying, he spent his nights before the tabernacle and united himself to Jesus in the Blessed Sacrament in order to obtain from God the conversion of India and Japan. "Da mihi animas. Lord, give me souls, souls," he used to repeat indefatigably.

Marie of the Incarnation, the great Canadian mystic and missionary, knew it well too. Her burning desire to be an apostle consumed her, and she stormed heaven to obtain the salvation of the pagans. "I embraced all the poor souls of the world," she said; "bearing them in my heart, I offered them to the Eternal Father, telling Him it was time He did justice to my divine spouse, to whom He had promised all the nations as His inheritance. I demanded them all for Jesus Christ, to whom by rights they belong."

Nearer to our time another Canadian, Marie St. Cecilia of Rome, exclaimed with ardent zeal, "Souls, souls, I want them all for God. I do not want one to escape the Redeemer. I want each of them to conform to his Creator's plan. I want to drown impious, blind hatred in pure love and atonement. I want to wash away iniquity in the blood of the divine Lamb. May God's will be done on earth as it is in heaven."[1]

5. It is a sublime but hard task to beg love for Christ. For if there are malleable, docile souls that receive kindly a soul that comes begging love, and listen willingly to her appeal, there are unfortunately so many others that bang the door in her face or pretend not to hear. There are

[1]Autobiography of Marie St. Cecilia of Rome, vol. 2, chapter 7, p. 82.

many that reply to the invitation by insults or obstinate refusals. How many useless and exhausting errands she must undertake, how many repeated attempts she must make with hardened souls. Perhaps she will knock a hundred times at the door of their hearts before they will open it and give a few crumbs of love for her Beloved Saviour.

But what do refusals, insults or even threats matter to her? She knows the worth, the eternal value of love. A mere "Yes" uttered unwillingly, perhaps, is a soul saved for ever, a soul that before long will spend eternity burning with love of God.

For her a little love is worth all the gold in the world. If so many men sail the seas to obtain a scrap of gold, what will she not do to obtain love? She would not change her profession of love's beggar for anything in the world, not even to become a queen and the admiration and envy of all.

Moreover, she has such joy each day in bringing what she has gained by her quest to Jesus, who hungers for love, such delight in being able to say, "Here, Beloved, is what I have won for You". Jesus is so kind and grateful, so interested in the story of her search. He encourages the soul so affectionately, applauds her success so happily. It is good to see His pleasure and await His smile. One smile from His divine lips is well worth a thousand days of toil and exhaustion.

6. Valiant souls who are messengers of the King of Love, your beggar's life is sublime. You well deserve the great joy that Jesus makes you feel in the depths of your heart, above all at certain times. You merit His divine tokens of affection, His intimate conversation and signs of love. Never get tired. If sometimes your begging expeditions do not produce the vast results desired, if they remain

for a long time sterile in appearance, think frequently of all the souls throughout the world that your prayers, ardent desires and self-sacrifice continually win for Jesus unknown to you. Remember that each soul saved means for Jesus an eternity of love.

Above all, do not forget that you are love's beggar for all eternity. The hour is approaching when you will go to heaven and see with admiration the real result of your quest for love, a marvellous and extremely consoling result. You will then continue your divine work with much more power and success. Love's beggar in eternity—you can even now joyfully exclaim with little St. Teresa, "I feel that my mission is about to begin, my task of making God loved as I love Him. I want to spend my heaven doing good on earth. I cannot take any rest till the end of the world. Then, when the angel says time is at an end, I shall take my rest. I shall be able to enjoy it, for the number of the elect will be complete." [1]

27. THE JOY OF HATING AND DESPISING SELF

1. At the beginning of the spiritual life, when our Lord gradually reveals to the soul the malice of her nature, and makes her see in it an ulcer or abscess always filling with filth, the soul experiences much repugnance at having to drink this chalice of interior humiliation. Our Lord will give her this chalice very often, in order gradually to detach her from self and make her die to all self-love.

If, however, the soul is generous and faithful, the day will come, after long years perhaps, when to her great

[1] *Story of a Soul*, chapter 12. Cf. also the *Autobiography of Marie St. Cecilia*, vol. 2, chapter 10, p. 102.

surprise she finds that the chalice of interior humiliation, of which she has so often drunk, is no longer bitter but delightful. Jesus in His great mercy has finally revealed, and taught her by a precious grace to appreciate, the strange mysterious joy of hating and despising self.

2. This joy is mysterious, perhaps the most mysterious of all those experienced by a soul united to Jesus. It is easy enough to understand that a soul inflamed with love of God should share His divine felicity, rejoice at the happiness of her Beloved, at His beauty, lovableness, almighty power. But to take pleasure in despising oneself, in discovering within oneself an abyss of wretchedness and sin, to find great joy in telling God and the heavenly court over and over again that one is nothing but a sinner, and to be happy at being ranked lowest of all, is a thing so contrary to nature as to seem almost incomprehensible. Only the blessed souls who have known by personal experience this uncommon joy can in fact understand it.

Such nevertheless is the joy experienced by a purified soul to whom God reveals her own indigence. Especially at the blessed moments when God infuses some degree of the passive humility that no amount of meditations could produce, the soul is exultant, like St. Francis Xavier, at discovering new weaknesses in herself, and at looking upon herself as an inexhaustible reservoir of malice and wickedness. Like the great Italian mystic Gemma Galgani, the soul pours forth long, loving, foolish expressions of humility. [1] With holy rapture she repeats the words of Job, "I have said to corruption, you are my father, and to worms, you are my mother and sister". [2]

---

[1] Cf. the *Letters and Ecstasies of Gemma Galgani*. They are filled with passionate expressions of humility.

[2] Job xvii. 14.

3. This strange hatred of self and this joy of seeing one-self unworthy of esteem, or love, which seem almost impossible to our nature full of self-love and self-complacency, are not an empty illusion. They are not the kind of imperfect fragile humility that disappears on contact with reality. They find expression in a thirst for external humiliation and feed on opprobrium, insults and calumny.

Think of the apparently foolish deeds of so many saints. Think of the humble Francis of Assisi begging not only his bread but also the insults of passers-by, enjoying the happiness of being taken for a fool and treated like one. Or of St. Ignatius, falsely accused of heresy, joyfully kissing the bars of his prison. Remember Angela of Foligno exclaiming: "I should like to go through cities and market places, with meat and fish tied round my neck, shouting, 'Here is a vile creature, full of malice and lies, seed of vice and evil' ". [1]

In order to glut this mysterious hatred, this holy con-tempt for self, the saints would like to be humiliated by everyone. They are never humiliated as much as they would like to be, never ranked as low as they want to be.

4. What is the secret of this strange joy and happiness which, like the Cross, is a scandal to the Gentiles and folly to the Jews? The secret is the intense pure love that inflames souls united to Jesus.

They passionately love God, whom they have seen to be supreme Beauty, indescribable loveliness, God whom they realise is above all created love. By that very fact they hate this wretched self that is in opposition to Him. They despise this sinful corrupt nature, endlessly swarm-ing with impure, egotistical and proud thoughts.

[1] Cf. Angela of Foligno, *Le livre des Visions*, traduit par Ernest Hello, Tralin, p. 60.

To love God and hate self are two complementary acts of one and the same love, which first considers God's loveliness in order to love Him unspeakably, then reflects on the supreme ugliness of self in order to hate it with full vigour. "Noverim me, noverim te. Oderim me, amem te", ardent souls exclaim with St. Augustine. "My God, may I know more and more Your entrancing loveliness that I may love it more and more. May I realise better the horror of my evil nature that I may hate it more implacably." One might say they love God with all the hate they have for self.

That is why the greater the joy they feel at seeing God great, powerful, beautiful, holy, the greater the happiness they have at seeing that *of themselves* they are ugly, proud, impure, and at understanding that the sinful self which has so often rebelled against their beloved God can no longer have any claim to the slightest esteem or affection.

5. If one wishes to analyse the matter further, and get to the root cause of this strange and holy hatred of self, it will be found in the fact that the loving soul has lost and abandoned self in order to live in God whom she loves. God has become her good, her joy, her treasure, the object of all her delight. Hence she looks upon the self she has rejected, no longer as her good, no longer as her own, but as a stranger, an enemy. That is what chiefly explains this mysterious hatred of self and the paradoxical joy taken by the soul in hating and despising self.

6. Or if one prefers to express it in this way, it is no longer merely the soul that lives and loves God and contemplates herself with hatred. It is Jesus who loves in her and by means of her, infusing in an eminent degree the theological virtue of charity by which God makes us share in His love, and by which God loves Himself in us.

Jesus, living fully and unfettered in the soul, imparts His own most pure and holy love of God. It is Jesus, with whom the soul is closely identified, who loves the divine perfections as His own and finds in them alone His satisfaction and happiness.

7. Who would not envy the souls that Jesus has set free and despoiled of self in order to associate them with the ineffable divine joy with which He loves God and Himself?

"May we too, Lord Jesus, one day be numbered among these blessed souls. May we merit by our generosity the special graces which will make our union and identification with You more and more intimate, and which will cause us one day to know by personal experience the joy that is hidden from so many souls, the joy of hating and despising self."

28. THE JOY OF LOVING ONE'S WRETCHEDNESS

1. We have seen that a soul possessed by divine love and in whom Jesus lives as He pleases finds real delight in hating and despising self. We will understand this strange joy even better if we examine this self-sacrificing love in one of its finest and most astonishing manifestations, love of one's own wretchedness.

Is it really possible to love one's wretchedness, the endlessly varied manifestations of the old Adam, our powerlessness, weaknesses, the subtle shifts of self-love, lack of docility to grace, our rebellious faults, the faults which despite our goodwill and repeated efforts find their way into our life and cause us pain? Is it really possible even for the most loving of souls to love such things and take delight in them? It is at least a paradox difficult to accept.

2. It must at once be admitted that we should not advise beginners in the spiritual life to love their own wretchedness. On the contrary, they must concentrate all their efforts on fighting energetically against the innumerable defects which are so many ramifications of self-love and constitute so many obstacles to progress towards perfection.

The situation is not the same for souls who have long struggled with tireless courage against the evil inclinations of their nature, and whom Jesus has led up the hard slopes of the purgative and illuminative ways to the life of union. Of course they too until the day of their death will fight valiantly against self-love which, as St. Francis de Sales said, only dies a quarter of an hour after we do. Nevertheless with them this struggle takes on a different aspect, for their life is concerned with the practices of the unitive life. In other words, their chief and constant preoccupation, as St. Thomas teaches, consists above all in living in God, adhering to Him, enjoying His divine perfections as though they were really their own.

The Divine Master gradually teaches such souls the great art of loving their wretchedness and of finding joy therein. He takes special care over it, because He knows that for them such love of their own ills constitutes the most effective way of fighting them and will lead them better than any other method to the perfection of disinterested love.

An eminent spiritual writer, Fr. Surin, remarks, ''This method (love of one's own abject state and wretchedness) causes in a week a more rapid advance in the purity of divine love and the uprooting of bad habits than anxious vigilance would bring in a whole year. One will easily be convinced of this if one has any experience in the ways of God."

3. For that matter, what are the faults of a generous soul in the life of union? They are surely nothing more than the involuntary weaknesses, slight faults, of which St. Teresa of the Child Jesus gracefully spoke. "I shall have the right, without offending God, to do these silly little things until my death, provided I remain humble and small. Look at little children, they are always breaking and tearing things and falling, yet they love their parents very much and are dearly loved by them." They are such things as lack of recollection or docility to grace, imperceptible glances at self, slight impatience and other involuntary faults. Such ills cause the soul both real pain and true joy. Pain certainly, because the soul would like to love God immensely, madly, with a love perfectly pure of all admixture of self. She would like to see and love only Him, and love Him, were it possible, from morning to night with actual and conscious love. But at the same time these faults cause the soul who has been taught by her Divine Master the precious love of her own abjection, an exquisite and intimate joy.

4. In order to gain some understanding of this mysterious joy, which is perhaps quite unknown to us, let us try to comprehend the sentiments of such a soul. Let us attentively weigh the thoughts that animate her and the motives that make her love her wretchedness. It will be the best way of arousing in ourselves a holy desire for this precious joy, and a means of preparing ourselves as far as we can for a happiness of which we had perhaps not even suspected the existence.

Taught by the interior Master, the soul united to God sees many reasons for loving the defects and failings that

God in His loving wisdom permits in her. For it is not without reason that she regards her ills as very useful friends. Let us ask her to explain the sentiments she feels and to tell us how she came by this strange love.

5. "First of all," she will say, "the faults that escape me humiliate my old enemy, this domineering self that seduced me so long and forced me, for all its vices, to love it. They abase the evil in my nature, the miserable self-love that used to cause me so much suffering, led me to commit so many faults and reduced me to real slavery. They unmask its ugliness and malice. How could I not rejoice to see it humiliated? I rejoice all the more because such joy itself enrages and confounds it.

"Furthermore, I love my ills because I find in such love the best means of making abundant reparation for them. Instead of being annoyed at them as I used to, out of self-love, I peacefully and joyfully humble myself, and rejoice at being nothing but a poor sinner. I give myself up to acts of repentant and trusting love of Him whom I have offended without really meaning to. I act like a little child that has saddened its mother. The child kisses and caresses her and shows her so much affection that the mother is quite delighted.

6. "Besides, these wretched faults are one of my greatest sources of wealth, so it is evident I must love them. Think of the graces they bring me day by day! Since Jesus taught me the great art of profiting by my faults, I ceaselessly display to God's merciful love my abjection and weakness. Far from being discouraged, I even put my trust in them! I know they are a sure means of touching the affectionate heart of my heavenly Father. I imitate those knowing beggars who shamelessly expose their deformities and repulsive sores the better to arouse pity. I know too that in a way God needs our wretched-

ness. Without it, He could not exercise His incomparable attribute of infinite mercy, of which Sacred Scripture says it is above all His other perfections.

"Then think of the gratitude I owe these ills! It is thanks to them that I have abandoned self in real earnest. It is long since I was a novice in the ways of the spirit, dreaming of curing this self of mine hopelessly full of malice, hoping fully to correct it. It is long since I dreamt of a sanctity which was to be a sort of ennobling of myself, entirely my own work, and in which I took secret self-satisfaction in advance. My repeated faults soon taught me I was on the wrong road, and made me understand that self was too wicked for anything perfect ever to be made of it. They taught me that whilst striving energetically to correct my faults, I must chiefly aim at forgetting and losing self, in order to find my joy, glory and treasure not in a perfected self, but in God. In other words, that God alone must be all in all to me.

"Since then I have found true happiness. I have surrendered to Jesus, so that He may rule in me, grow in me while I decrease, so that He may be my holiness on the ruins of my self-love. I will never love sufficiently my own wretchedness that has set me free, and led me gently to life in God and union with Jesus.

7. "Finally and above all my ills fill me with joy because they set off in more brilliant contrast the perfections of my Beloved Lord. For God chooses to alternate in me the sentiment of my indigence with His divine consolations, in order to reveal in turn my immeasurable poverty and His infinite riches, my indescribable ugliness and His beauty that transports the angels in an eternal ecstasy of love. In this way the very contrast between my faults and the divine perfections throws into bolder relief the divine attributes and makes me understand and appreciate

better the unsuspected treasures of the God whom I now possess as my own good. Each fault is like a flash of lightning in the night, opening my eyes to endless vistas of divine perfection. Is there any wonder that my faults fill me with very pure joy?''

It is evident, therefore, that the soul's many ills make her come out of herself and gradually lead her to the heights of perfect love. Each failing is an occasion for acts of pure love, love more and more disinterested. That is why all the signs of her abjection are dear to her. The poor soul is devoured by divine love, consumed with the desire to love God more intensely and above all more purely, with a love that is more and more unselfish. Yet she languishes in her own helplessness. Then it is that her own ills console her and come to her assistance. Each of them gives occasion for a perfect act of love of God and of intense contempt of self.

It would be a good thing to ruminate often on these thoughts, especially in times of consolation, when our soul seems to burn with love of God. Perhaps in this way, helped by a special grace, we would come to feel in a more perceptible manner the precious joy of loving our own abjection. Then we too would learn by experience how much such joy helps us to advance in the way of pure love. We would then ask it of God insistently.

8. We have tried to analyse, and display the causes of the joy felt by the generous soul that loves her own abjection. It is hardly necessary to mention that it is often a long time before the soul herself realises what these causes are, for she does not usually reason out her love and joy. For the most part she feels such joy spontaneously, almost instinctively, as a result of her ardent love of God. However, at certain times, one or other advantage of her own

wretchedness strikes her more vividly, some sentiment of humility, love or trust awakened by the sight of her abjection makes itself felt more intensely. Gradually the soul builds up a store of habitual thoughts and sentiments called forth sometimes distinctly, but usually in a confused manner, by the sight of her own wretchedness.

Moreover, this joy is so spiritual, and presupposes such a pure love of God, that usually it is not emotionally felt. It is only in times of divine visitation, in exquisite moments of passive love, that the soul comes to feel this sublime joy in a more perceptible form.

All the saints have experienced this remarkable joy, for it is a fruit of ardent love of God. Few have mentioned it explicitly in their writings and this is perhaps why many people have never read or heard of it. With the exception of the lovable St. Francis de Sales, nobody, in our opinion, has described it as accurately and as insistently as St. Teresa of the Child Jesus. We will be permitted, therefore, to glean in her writings a few of the numerous thoughts in which this joy and love of one's own wretchedness are more vividly expressed. These extracts will lead to a better understanding of this mysterious joy, unsuspected even by many fervent souls, and will make more familiar the thoughts and sentiments proper to awaken it.

9. Shortly after her entry into Carmel, when she was only sixteen, Teresa, taught by the Holy Ghost, had already understood the great advantages to be derived from love of one's own abjection. She wrote to her sister Céline as follows: "We must not think we can have love without suffering. We have our nature, it isn't there for nothing. What treasures it helps us to acquire ! It is our bread-winner. It is so precious that Jesus came down on earth in order to possess it. We should like to suffer

generously, intensely; we would like never to fall—
what an illusion! What does it matter if I am continually
falling? It makes me feel my own weakness and I find
great profit in that. 'My God, You see what I can do if
you do not carry me in Your arms. If You leave me to
myself it must be because You choose to see me on the
ground. So why should I worry?'"[1]

A few years later in her autobiography she wrote the
following lines. They provoke thought. "At the beginning of my spiritual life, about the age of thirteen or
fourteen, I wondered what I would achieve later. I
thought I perfectly understood what perfection is. I
soon recognised that the more one advances, the further
one thinks oneself from the goal. Now I am resigned to
seeing myself always imperfect. I even find joy in
it."[2]

Later she returns to the same thought. "It is possible
that later I may appear to myself even more full of ills,
but I'm no longer surprised at anything. I don't grieve at
seeing myself weakness itself. On the contrary, I glory
in it and expect every day to discover new faults in
myself. I confess that such light on my own nothingness
does me more good than light on faith."[3]

She wrote as follows to her cousin Marie Guérin.
"You are mistaken, my dear, if you think your Teresa
is ardently walking the path of sacrifice. She is weak,
very weak, and every day she realises it by bitter and
salutary experience. But Jesus is pleased to teach her the
art of glorying in her infirmities. That is a great grace
and I beg Him to give you it, for calm and peace of mind
are to be found in that sentiment. When one sees oneself

[1] Letter 5 to her sister Céline.
[2] *Story of a Soul*, chapter 7.
[3] Ibid., chapter 9.

so miserable, one can no longer esteem self, one looks only to the Beloved."[1]

This passage shows that according to St. Teresa, love of one's wretchedness is a great grace that is to be had much more by prayer than by reasoning.

Her last illness above all was an opportunity for the saint to show her love of her abjection, and the joy it gave her. One day when she felt very weak, she had shown slight annoyance at not being understood. She immediately called back the nurse and said, with tears in her eyes, "I'm sorry". A few minutes afterwards she told an intimate friend, "How happy I am to feel I am so imperfect, and to have so much need of the mercy of God at the moment of death".[2]

Shortly before her death she said, in answer to a question, "Many weaknesses befall me, but I'm delighted at them. Nor am I always above trifling earthly things. For example, I'm upset about some foolish thing I have said or done. Then I enter into myself and say, 'Alas, I'm still at the first stages as I used to be!' But I think that very gently, without sadness. It is agreeable to feel weak and small."[3]

Finally we will quote the well-known letter which she wrote during her illness to her sister Mother Agnes. We should like to be able to quote this magnificent letter in full.

While the saint was suffering from a severe attack of fever, she was asked to sit for a painting. Momentarily her face betrayed her interior conflict. In the evening she wrote the letter from which we quote, and which finishes with these heartfelt words, followed by her

[1] Letter 2 to Marie Guérin.
[2] Novissima Verba, 29 July.
[3] Ibid., 5 July.

famous prophecy. "When I returned to our cell, I wondered what Jesus had thought of me. At once I
remembered what He said one day to the woman taken
in adultery: 'Has anyone condemned you?' With tears in
my eyes I replied to Him, 'No one, Lord, neither my
little Mother, the image of your affection, nor my sister,
the image of Your justice.' I feel sure I can go in peace,
for He will not condemn me either.

"O beloved Mother, I admit I am much happier at
having been impatient than if, helped by grace, I had
been a model of patience. It does me so much good to
see that Jesus is just as gentle and affectionate to me.
Really it is enough to make one die of gratitude and love.

"Little Mother, you will understand that this evening
the vase of divine mercy has overflowed for your child.
Even now I recognise that all my hopes will be fulfilled.
The Lord will do wonderful things for me that will
infinitely surpass my immense desires." [1]

29. JOYFUL LOVE OF ONE'S OWN INSIGNIFICANCE

1. The soul united to God finds happiness, as we have
seen, in loving all her ills. We shall have no difficulty in

[1]Letter 8 to Mother Agnes of Jesus.

N.B.—On the joy of loving one's wretchedness and also the joy of
loving one's littleness (see the following pages) one can meditate with
profit the whole of the excellent chapter 5, entitled "Humility", in
L'esprit d'enfance de la bienheureuse Thérèse de l'Enfant-Jésus.

One will also find in the fine autobiography of Mother St. Cecilia
of Rome (Couvent de Jesus-Marie, Sillery, P.Q., Canada, 1934),
noble expressions of the love of one's wretchedness, nothingness, etc.
Cf. for example, vol. 2, chapter 4, pp. 41-42; chapter 7, p. 82, etc.

understanding, therefore, that she also loves her weakness, littleness, nothingness, and rejoices in them.

Pursued by divine love, she has come to see and love nothing in the world but God. God alone counts in her eyes. She loves Him now quite exclusively. Everything else on earth, including herself, is only loved by her in God, as a manifestation in the created order of the divine perfections. That is why her jealous love of God finds much joy in reflecting that the God she loves as her only good is all and that all the rest is nothing, that He is Being itself and that all creatures exist only in Him and by Him.

Everything that extols and magnifies God is most pleasing to her, as well as everything that lessens creatures and reduces them to their true proportions. If anything could pain her, it would certainly be to find that God is not all, that there is even one single thing independent of Him. But she knows quite well that such is not the case and could never be. The famous words that God used to St. Catherine of Siena delight her, "I am He who is, you are she who is not". These words defend the honour of God, from whom so many men by their pride and self-satisfaction tend to steal the glory that is His due.

2. Souls filled with proud self-love take delight and glory in extolling self, admiring their talents, thinking themselves great and courageous. On the contrary, a soul emptied of self by the love of God finds happiness in feeling her own weakness, nothingness, incapacity for good. She no longer has any glory of her own. She would consider it an abominable theft, as well as an absurdity, wilfully to admit the slightest thought of vainglory and self-complacency about the gifts that God has freely bestowed on her. Her glory is in God's own glory, the infinite changeless glory that the three divine Persons

give each other, and which no creature can ever diminish. It is the magnificent symphony of heavenly praise which innumerable angels and saints sing unceasingly to God, a distant echo of which was enough to ravish in ecstasy the ardent soul of a Joseph of Cupertino. It is the wonderful harmony of the immense hymn of love which in union with all the members of His mystical body Jesus sings on earth to the glory of the Blessed Trinity. That is what the loving soul glories in, an incomparable glory, which satisfies the needs of her heart a thousand times over. Beside it, the praise of men, of which she used to dream, seems ridiculously mean and despicable.

3. Our self-love causes us to find intimate satisfaction in telling ourselves that we owe such and such a success to our own industry, that we have acquired such and such a virtue by our own efforts. On the contrary, a soul consumed by divine love likes to think that it is grace that has done everything, that her own share has only been to spoil the divine work to a greater or less degree, and to hinder the full development of Christ's life in her. She takes great delight in owing her wretched self nothing except contempt, and in owing everything to God, whom she loves. The saying of the great saint of Siena delights her. "The only perfect things in us are what God operates in us without us." Consequently she experiences particular satisfaction in being able to thank God for all the good she sees in herself or that she has done for others.

St. Teresa of the Child Jesus was so penetrated with these sentiments that vanity had become practically impossible to her. She could quite truthfully say, "I am too small now to be vain, too small to be able to compose fine phrases in order to make people think I am very humble. I prefer to admit that the Almighty has done great things in me, and the greatest of them is to have shown me my littleness, and my powerlessness to do good.''

She liked to say she owed everything to God and expected nothing from her works and her so-called good deeds. She called them a wealth that corrupts when one takes self-satisfaction in them. To a nun who was terrified of God's judgement, she said, ''There is only one way of forcing God not to judge us at all, which is to come before Him empty-handed''. That is what she wanted to do herself. Counting for nothing her heroic life, she aimed not at gaining heaven by her good works, but at stealing into it like the Holy Innocents or the Good Thief, who went straight to heaven simply by divine mercy.

4. The love of God makes us delight in loving our nothingness and insignificance. Humility does so too. A soul united to Jesus burns to humiliate and belittle self as much as possible. In this she is powerfully stimulated by the immense condescension of God, who, though All, chose to descend to our nothingness and live among us. By Holy Communion and sanctifying grace He still lowers Himself to us with astonishing familiarity. Above all, the Incarnation, that masterpiece of divine condescension and humility, urges her on unceasingly. She knows that God, not being able to find in His infinite nature any reasons or means of humbling Himself, chose, in His ineffable love for His creatures, to borrow from our human nature these reasons and means. Infinitely rich in all other virtues, He wished to produce what was apparently impossible, and by taking our nature, to become rich in humility as well.

Inevitably a humble soul will burn with insatiable desire to humble herself in return, in order to respond to

so much condescending love and so much divine
humility. That is why she is not only resigned to being
nothing, but loves it. She takes delight in being very
little before God. Everything that makes her feel more
clearly her own nothingness fills her with joy.

5. Yet she will never be, and never feel, as small as she
would like to. Her desire to respond not too inadequately
to the unheard of self-abasement of God will never be
satisfied. How far can she humble herself? Can she in
fact abase herself at all? To descend to her own nothingness, and recognise her complete poverty, is scarcely
really to abase herself. It is only to return to the truth
of things, come down from the heights of pride to her
true level, and simply recognise the nothingness and sin-
fulness of her nature. God alone, the Infinite, was ever
able to abase Himself, that is, to descend lower than what
He is.

What can the soul do in her incapacity to humble and
abase herself as she would like to? She will find joy in
the very sentiment of her incapacity.

Incapable of glorifying God by self-abasement as she
would like to, she is happy that this incapacity itself
glorifies the Lord, by manifesting her nothingness.
Moreover, it abases her more than she could abase herself.
In other words the soul in her unquenchable thirst for
humility delights at feeling herself in a bottomless pit of
baseness and poverty by her very incapacity to glorify
God and humble herself.

This is what Ruysbroeck described so well. "A
humble man," he said, "will never place God high
enough or himself low enough. But here is the marvel:
his powerlessness will turn into wisdom and the
defectiveness of his necessarily inadequate action will, in
his eyes, become the greatest delight of his life."

Elsewhere he writes, "In face of God, too immense to be worthily honoured by us, we must feel in our act of adoration the pleasure of our powerlessness. Even if every man gave at every moment as much glory to God as all men and angels put together, the spirit of adoration would still not be satisfied. But humility, if we can only engulf ourselves therein, gives us some satisfaction."

6. A soul intimately united to Jesus also loves and delights in her insignificance because it is a sure means of pleasing God and obtaining divine grace.

St. Teresa of Lisieux, that perfect model of love of her own littleness, has thrown much light on this truth. In her magnificent sixteenth letter to her sister Marie of the Sacred Heart, she wrote, "I beg you to understand that in order to love Jesus and be His victim of love, one is all the more apt for acts of consuming and transforming love in proportion as one is weak and miserable. The mere desire to be a victim suffices, but we must consent always to remain poor and feeble. That is what is difficult, for where will be found true poverty of spirit? It is far to find, says the author of the *Imitation*. He did not say one must seek for it among great souls. He said far away, that is, in baseness, nothingness. Therefore let us stay far from brilliant things. Let us love our little-ness, love to feel nothing. Let us love our littleness, then we will be poor in spirit and Jesus will come and seek us, however far away we may be, and will transform us into a flame of love."

In connection with her ardent and apparently un-realisable desire of becoming a real saint, St. Teresa used the pleasant image of a lift. "I should also like to find a lift to raise me to Jesus, for I am too small to climb the steep stair of perfection. Then I sought in Holy Scripture some indication of the lift I desired. I found

these words spoken by the mouth of Eternal Wisdom
Himself, 'Suffer little children to come unto Me. . . . I
will console you as a mother caresses her child, I will
carry you at My breast and dandle you on My knees.'

"Never did more affectionate harmonious words
delight my soul. 'Your arms, Jesus, are the lift that will
raise me to heaven.' For that I have no need to grow. On
the contrary, I must remain small, or rather become
smaller and smaller."[1]

7. In conclusion, let us add that love of our insignificance
not only makes us joyfully taste our own nothingness, but
also gives the soul the changeless peace of perfect trust
and the calm joy of holy spiritual childhood.

Convinced as she is of her total incapacity to do anything that is good, the soul expects nothing from self and
naturally comes to entrust herself for everything to the
care of her heavenly Father. She lives with Him in great
intimacy like a little child. The lovable sentiments of
childhood soon become quite natural to her. Above all,
her trust in God continually increases, for the less she
expects from her own nothingness, the more she hopes
for from the almighty love of her heavenly Father. This
trust even becomes instinctive, as it is with children, and
through all the vicissitudes of life, the soul sleeps in
peace in the arms of God.

Here again it is sufficient to quote little St. Teresa.
By a graceful simile she makes us grasp the relation
between love of one's littleness and the spiritual childhood of which she has given such charming examples.

"To remain small is to recognise one's nothingness
and wait for everything from God, as a little child expects
everything from its father. It is not to worry about anything, and not enrich oneself. Even with poor people the

[1]*Story of a Soul*, chapter ix.

very small child is given what it needs. But when he has grown up, his father no longer wants to provide him with food, and tells him to go and work and support himself. Well, I don't want ever to hear such words. That is why I have never wanted to grow up, for I feel incapable of gaining my living—the eternal life of heaven."[1]

Nothing can disturb the joyous peace caused by love of our insignificance and the spirit of childhood. Speaking of her aridity and her difficulties in prayer due to sleepiness, the saint remarked, "I ought not to be pleased with my aridity, but attribute it to my lack of fervour and fidelity. I ought to be sad at often falling asleep during my prayers or thanksgiving. Well, I'm not sad. I remember that little children are just as pleasing to their parents when they are asleep as when they are awake. Besides I know that the Lord sees our weakness and is mindful that we are but dust."[2]

30. THE JOY OF PRAISING GOD

1. The praise of God plays an important part in the life of all good Christians but more especially in the life of priests, monks and nuns who read the Breviary or spend a large part of the day singing Divine Office.

The Breviary or Divine Office from beginning to end is praise of God. The magnificent psalms that form as it were its marrow, are nothing else but a continual praise and glorification of the divine perfections. The psalmist never tires of extolling these perfections, above all,

[1] *Advice and memories.*

[2] *Story of a Soul*, chapter viii.

God's power and mercy. "Domine, Dominus noster, quam admirabile est nomen tuum in universa terra. Quoniam elevata est magnificentia tua super caelos"[1] (Ps. 8). "Benedicite, omnia opera Domini, Domino. Laudate et superexaltate eum in saecula"[2] (Cant. trium puerorum).

2. To this continual homage paid to the divine perfections, humble adoration and boundless admiration, the praise of God also adds a cry of unceasing gratitude. A truly grateful soul spontaneously breaks forth into praise. She exhausts all her capacity in blessing the Lord. "Confitebor tibi, Domine, in toto corde meo quoniam audisti verba oris mei"[3] (Ps. 137). "Benedictus Dominus Deus Israel, quia visitavit et fecit redemptionem plebis suae"[4] (Cant. Zachar.).

3. But praise is also and above all a love-song. This is unfortunately too often forgotten. Praise only attains its perfection, full value and beauty, and blossoms into joy, on the lips of a loving soul. In praising her Beloved she experiences intense happiness which at times becomes a holy intoxication of jubilation. Praise for her is only the ardent inexhaustible and ever-varying expression of her love of God. She satisfies her love by singing the perfections of God, extolling with all His creatures His entrancing beauty, His infinite power, tireless mercy and incomprehensible wisdom. That for her is simple, intense, complete love.

[1]"O Lord our Lord, how admirable is Thy name in the whole earth! For thy magnificence is elevated above the heavens."

[2]"Bless the Lord, all ye works of the Lord. Praise and exalt Him above all for ever."

[3]"I will praise Thee, O Lord, with my whole heart, for thou hast heard the words of my mouth."

[4]"Blessed be the Lord God of Israel, because He hath visited and wrought the redemption of His people."

4. This love-song is essentially a song of joy and gladness. What happiness a soul in love with God feels when she pours out loving praises, rivalling the heavenly court in blessing and glorifying her Beloved in endlessly different ways. "Venite exsultemus Domino, jubilemus Deo salutari nostro"[1] (Ps. 94). "Laetabor et exsultabo in te, psallam nomini tuo, Altissime"[2] (Ps. 9).

Excess of love overflows in praise and loving jubilation.

The loving soul that praises God is happy, all the happier because her praises are not vain, lying flattery. She has no fear of overstepping truth by exaggerated praise, as earthly lovers do. She knows that in glorifying God in the most exalted and magnificent terms, she will say no more than the truth, or, rather, will never be adequate to God's reality, whatever she says. Her divine Beloved is lovable beyond all thought of praise, and the most ardent hymns of love will never be anything but a lifeless, inadequate sketch of God's wonders.

5. Finally, the praise of God is a joyous song of glory, a proud song of triumph for the truly loving soul. She has long since renounced all personal glory. Full of horror for self, whose innumerable ills God has gradually revealed to her, she has nothing but repugnance for any glory creatures could give her. Their lying praises fill her with shame and seem like affronts, insults. Yet if she has lost her own glory, she finds it a hundredfold in God. The Lord is her glory and in Him is her delight. In place of self she loves God, infinitely lovable and worthy of all praise, and He fills her with holy self-respect and pride in Him.

---

[1]"Come let us praise the Lord with joy, let us joyfully sing to God our saviour."

[2]"I will be glad and rejoice in thee: I will sing to Thy name, O Thou, Most High."

F*

How base the flattery of worldly people now seems to
the soul. Who could ever be compared to her beloved
Lord? Beside His surpassing loveliness all earthly beauty
is mere ugliness. Beside His omniscience all created wisdom is folly. Beside His infinite power the power of the
greatest rulers is but weakness. The soul is proud of her
Beloved, proud with immense pride. It is with a sentiment of happy and very disinterested glory that she
breaks forth before all the world into loving praise, or
loses herself in contemplation of the divine perfections.
6. Very few, unfortunately, fully know the happiness of
praising God, and know how to feed thereon. Too many
souls see in this praise only a respectful but cold adoration
of God's perfections, or gratitude for His innumerable
benefactions. They do not realise its chief attraction and
delight, the ardent expression and disinterested happiness
of pure love. Praise has not yet become for them what it
ought primarily to be, an exercise of pure love of the
God of all perfection, who is not only most holy and
almighty, but also the Beloved, chosen out of thousands,
her only good, her all in all.[1]

Love God, faithful soul, and sing your love in praises
ever new, and you also will enjoy the happiness and pride
of praising God. Divine Office will be transformed for
you, becoming a source of pure delight unknown before.
Delectare in Domino. You will learn in it lovingly to
take delight in the Lord.

In order, however, to love and praise God, unite yourself to Jesus. Only then will your praise and the joy
flowing from it be perfect. Often recall to mind that He

---

[1]Ardent souls like Elizabeth of the Trinity (who liked to call herself "laus gloriae") and Marie of the Trinity (Consummata) had well
understood the beauty of praising God. Consequently they found
nexhaustible and ever fresh happiness in singing the praises of God.

lives in you, that He longs to glorify His Father in you and by you. Give Him the great joy of being able to use your heart and lips to extol His holy, loving Father. What enviable joy, intimate satisfaction and heavenly peace you will find in praising with Jesus, and on His behalf, His Beloved Father. Having found a heart that allows Him freely to act as He pleases, Jesus will be delighted to do so. In you and thanks to you He will indulge to His heart's content in praise of God. The joy you will feel will only be the repercussion of His own divine joy, the mysterious radiance of His happiness, satisfaction and divine content.

31. JOY IN THE CONSCIOUSNESS OF GOD'S PRESENCE

1. The soul that devotes herself generously to the spiritual life gradually detaches herself from all creatures and finally gathers all her powers into an *active* loving attention, as constant as she can make it, to God present in her. She knows by faith that God, whom she is striving to love exclusively, dwells within her by sanctifying grace. Conscious of the infinite treasure she possesses, she ceaselessly turns to Him. On the model of St. Catherine of Siena, she makes in the depth of her heart an oratory in which, like Mary Magdalen, she loves to rest at the feet of the Divine Master.

God usually does not let such generosity go unrewarded for long. The time comes when He carries out the promise He made at the Last Supper. "If anyone love Me, My Father and I will love him and will come to him and take up Our abode in him." He gives the soul the gift of infused passive prayer. At times He grants her a *passive* loving attention to Him. Often too He adds a very special sentiment which has been termed the consciousness or sense of the divine presence.

2. What precisely is this mystical sense of presence? Much has been written about it without full agreement being reached. We need not at present concern ourselves with a full and precise definition of it. What is certain is that it is a special, passive, infused sentiment, very different from the active sense of the divine presence which can be had as a consequence of reasoning and efforts to recollect oneself. It is a gratuitous gift of God, quite beyond our scope, which gives us without any reflection on our part the clear sense that God is present in the centre of our soul. We feel, often with great pleasure, that the Master is there. "Magister adest et vocat te. The Master is there and is calling you." We have a quasi-experimental knowledge of His presence, as it were an intuition or direct awareness of it. We feel at the same time that this interior guest loves us dearly, that He is in love with us and we with Him. "Dilectus meus mihi et ego illi (Cant. ii. 16). My Beloved is mine and I am His. Inveni quem diligit anima mea, tenui eum nec dimittam (Cant. iii. 4). I have found, exclaims the soul favoured with this grace, Him whom my soul loves. I have found Him, I love Him and will not let Him go."

The soul would like always to remain with Him in this way, and never let Him go. With the Apostle Peter she would gladly say, "Lord, it is good for us to be here. Let us build three tabernacles." Suddenly, however, the Beloved is no longer there. The soul no longer feels His presence. He has gone as suddenly as He came. How had He come, how has He gone? Ubi declinavit dilectus tuus? (Cant. v. 17). The soul does not know. The one thing certain is that He is no longer there and no longer delights the soul by the charm of His presence.

It would be very difficult for a soul that has never had the experience to imagine just what this mystical presence of God is, which enters the soul, imbuing her with a love that is both God's and her own. On the other hand, those who know it by experience make no mistake about it. This sense of God's presence is unique.

No doubt when conversing with her Beloved Guest the soul had very often felt joyous peace and transports of ardent love. But such sentiments were to a large extent the effect of her own activity, very different from the passive supernatural sense of God's presence which the Lord in His infinite liberality has now bestowed.

3. This sense of the divine presence imbues the soul with joy and peace of a new kind, unknown to her before, in comparison with which all the joys she has experienced till now seem very slight and faint. She has become the chosen tabernacle of God. She has heaven on earth.

Let us ask the great contemplative of Avila what she thinks of the joy of such a soul. "As soon as she arrives at this stage," she said, "the soul begins to lose all desire for earthly things, and that without difficulty. For she sees clearly that not a single moment of such bliss can be had here below, and that no riches, power, honours or pleasures could suffice to procure it for a single instant. To my mind it is impossible that such bliss should be had from earthly joys, for they are never unmixed, whereas during the space of this prayer the delight is pure and untroubled. The sadness comes later when we see the favour is over, without our being able to recover it. Even if one were to tear oneself to pieces with penances, prayers and other such things, it would be of no avail if the Lord Himself does not wish to bestow the favour."[1]

St. Francis de Sales, after describing the happiness of the soul peacefully enjoying the delicate sense of God's presence within her, concludes as follows: "No, the soul thus at peace in God would not leave this repose for anything in the world".[2]

4. This joy in the felt presence of God is very dear to the soul. It is valued as a great treasure. For, as we have seen, God not only makes the soul perceive that He is within her, but also that He dearly loves her. The soul no longer needs to convince herself, by reflection, of God's immense love. She feels it. A child whose mother pressed it tenderly to her heart would surely not doubt her love. The soul who enjoys God's caresses in this manner can never have any doubt of His ardent unitive love for her. In return she is totally imbued with love for Him.

Consequently it is not surprising that these joys of mystical love awaken in the soul an insatiable desire to enjoy again and again the presence of her Beloved, and to tell Him of her love over and over again. The soul that has once drunk at this heavenly fountain thirsts always to drink from it. The thirst only increases. Soon the desire to enjoy the presence of God, whom she loves, and to possess Him by unitive love, becomes the centre as it were of her spiritual life, the force that impels all her activity. She sees everything in that light. She does everything to be united to God and to possess Him.

To urge herself on to virtue, mortification, abnegation, humility, zealous charity, complete trust and confidence, the soul no longer needs a variety of stimulants. She only needs to feel or even remember Jesus present in the

---

[1] St. Teresa, *Autobiography*, chapter xiv.

[2] *Treatise on the Love of God*, Book VI, chapter 8.

centre of her heart. Perhaps at that very moment Jesus makes His presence perceptible and says to her, "Give Me your heart, love Me as I love you". How could she, a poor weak creature, refuse a fibre of her heart to the great God who loves her and begs her love? For His sake in future all suffering and toil will be a pleasure. So will the practice of all the virtues, for however they differ, they all imply love, of which they are but different forms. They are means of pleasing the Beloved and becoming more and more closely united to Him.

5. What seems most precious to the soul in this longed-for sense of God's presence is that she sees it is the supreme and only true means of satisfying her need of ceaseless union with God and uninterrupted loving attention to Him.

In her desire always to love more and in a more perfect way, the soul would like always to be thinking of her Beloved, always telling Him of her love. She seeks and finds God everywhere, in everything. Everything speaks to her of God and His divine perfections, everything sings of His love for her and invites her to love Him in return. Very often each day she lovingly glances up at Him, with an ardent aspiration. Even that does not satisfy her. She regretfully reproaches herself with the rare moments when her capricious imagination wanders away from Him. Her nature is still there, and therefore she stops thinking of her Divine Beloved.

What can she do to realise her dream of continual loving attention to God? There is only one means, an excellent and infallible means, which is, to obtain from Jesus the grace for His presence to become more and more perceptible, even uninterruptedly, if He so imparts the sense of His beloved presence.

When the Divine Saviour does so, no effort is needed

for the soul to remain in His dear presence. At such
times Jesus seems to hold her by the hand beside Him.
How could she lose sight of Him? Even the most dis-
tracting and absorbing occupations do not separate her
from Him. She performs them in His company, for the
Master can make her feel His presence just as plainly
amid the works of active life as in the calm of peaceful
contemplation.

That is the chief reason for the soul's constant great
desire always to enjoy His divine company. She is not in
fact moved by a selfish desire even for the purely spiritual
joys that the sense of His presence brings. She would
willingly renounce them if she could keep the precious
sense of presence itself, for she sees this to be the only
means of fully satisfying her need of thinking of God
always, of doing everything in Him, with Him and for
Him, and of remaining always in actual union with
Him.

The soul is indeed enviable whom God leads to the
blessed heights of perfect transforming union, where she
sees her desires perfectly fulfilled. God grants her the
uninterrupted sense of his presence, fills her so completely, and lives in her with such plenitude, that at every
moment she maintains without difficulty the consciousness of His divine company.

6. One might think, from what we have said, that the
sense of God's presence is always pleasurable and fills the
soul with great joy. Such, however, is not the case. The
Divine Master varies His gifts in many ways, according to
the needs of the soul and His plans for her.

Usually at the beginning He only grants this sense
during prayer and for a relatively short time. Then the
sentiment of Presence is very joyous and affects the
emotions. Jesus knows that a soul accustomed to the

coarser pleasures of created things could not properly
appreciate the more refined pleasure of purely spiritual
delight. Therefore He gives the soul less refined joys.
Later this emotional pleasure gradually disappears, at
least as a general rule, making way for a purely spiritual
joy in the very centre of the soul. But even this joy, if
intense, sometimes overflows into the emotions, though
not in the same way as at the beginning.

The joy and delight caused by Jesus' presence is often
peaceful, calm as a still stream with almost imperceptible
current. The soul lovingly rests on the breast of her
Beloved, finding very little to say to Him. Sometimes,
on the contrary, this joy is impetuous, enraptured, like a
stream leaping down among boulders. The soul is then
jubilant and pours out her joy in expressions of love,
called forth by her need to manifest her passionate
attachment to Jesus.

Sometimes the presence of God or of Jesus Christ, the
Word made Flesh,[1] manifests itself by an intimate spiritual
embrace that irradiates the soul with love. Then the
words of the Canticle are fulfilled, "Laeva ejus sub capite
meo et dextera illius amplexabitur me" (Cant. ii. 6).

Often, however, it is not pleasurable and delightful,
but arid. The soul is conscious of God's presence, and
that is all. St. Jeanne de Chantal experienced this
condition for many years, and suffered much by it.

Furthermore, the sense of God's presence varies con-
siderably in intensity. Often it is scarcely perceptible
and the soul does not quite know whether her Divine
Guest is keeping her company or not. At other times it
is very vivid, so vivid that it absorbs almost all her attention. The soul finds it difficult to attend to her ordinary

[1]Often it is God without distinction of person who makes the
soul feel His presence, but often it is Jesus Christ the Word.

work and while doing so she is still united in affection to Jesus.

A distinction is also drawn between what is known as quietude in prayer, and active quietude. God can make His presence perceptible during prayer. That is the usual case. He can also do so during our actions, and keep us united to Him amid our work, meals, recreation.

It must be noted also that usually God manifests His presence in the depth of the soul, and focusses her powers there, as honey attracts a swarm of bees. But He can likewise manifest His presence near or around us. The soul then feels herself engulfed as it were in an ocean of love. God makes her feel His charm, lovableness, beauty, goodness. How? The soul hardly knows. She does not see Him, she senses He is there, that she loves Him. Sometimes she would like to leave self as it were to throw herself before Him.

A great contemporary mystic, known under the pseudonym of Lucie-Christine, describes as follows the double sense of God's presence around and in the soul, in its vivid form. "For two days now God gives me every time I go to church, a sense of His presence which I find very difficult to describe, for it seems to be above concepts. It is something seen, though it has no visible shape. It is both sight and union. I am engulfed in God, I see Him, so that my soul is more certain she sees Him, and is more affected thereby, than my bodily eyes are by the light of day. At the same time He is in me, one with me. He penetrates me, He is more intimately present than the air I breathe. He is more united to me than the soul is united to the body to which it gives life. I am absorbed by Him, I no longer know with what existence I exist, I seem to be transported into another life, into a region that is no longer this earth. This detachment is ineffable, a rapture, intoxicating. The soul knows God as no word could make Him known, and there results a burning thirst to make all souls prostrate themselves before Him."[1]

Such are some of the innumerable varieties of the sense of God's presence. The Divine Master chooses as He pleases, according to His plans. For, as we must never forget, He is supremely free and His liberality knows no laws.

7. Let us add that the simple sense of the presence of God, or of Jesus Christ the Word, may also be accompanied by that of His life and action in us. This is chiefly the case in the higher stages of union, in the case of the soul that has passed through the night of the spirit and is approaching transforming union. She not only feels that Jesus the Divine Word is present within her to receive the homage of her love, but also that He is living and active in her. She feels that her transports of love are nothing else than the flames of divine charity, the love with which Jesus in her and by her loves His Father. This causes her a great desire to let Jesus act freely in her, to be identified with Him by a life of perfect self-surrender.

Lucie-Christine describes this sense of the transforming action of Jesus within us in the following terms. "God takes possession of my whole being by this embrace. It is no longer I who am there, it is He. I no longer see myself, I see only Jesus. I am not destroyed, but His life takes possession of me, dominates and absorbs me. On my knees, I no longer recognise myself, I see only the Son of God really and sacramentally present

[1]Cf. *Journal Spirituel de Lucie-Christine*, edited by A. Poulain, S.J., pp. 199-200. We quote it also in our *Anthologie Mystique*, pp. 329-330.

(in Holy Communion). I adore Him, but the divine
action penetrates and transforms my adoration. The
Divine Being thinks, lives, and loves in me, I have no
longer any life save through Him. As the apostle said,
"Now I live, not I, but Christ lives in me".[1]

This transforming action of Jesus in the soul grows
unceasingly and the soul finally reaches the highest degree
of the spiritual and mystical life, transforming union, also
known as mystical marriage. The sense of the presence
and action of God in the soul has become continuous and
never leaves her. Moreover, it develops into a distinct
awareness of the Three Persons of the Blessed Trinity.
The soul experiences in a special way the Father, Son
and Holy Spirit. Henceforward she performs all her
actions in the company of these beloved Guests. Or
rather, God performs them in her and by her, for in a
certain manner He deifies the soul and makes her share
unceasingly in the life of the Trinity, in the infinite love
with which He loves Himself in the Trinity of His
Persons.

8. We must leave to the loving wisdom of God the care
of granting us the mystical grace of the sense of His
presence when and as He wills.

That does not mean we cannot desire it and even ask
for it, if up to now we have not been favoured with it.
The great mystical writers, following in this the doctrine
of St. John of the Cross, agree in saying that whilst it
would be dangerous to desire and ask for the exterior
manifestations of the mystical life (which are only its
accessories), visions, revelations, the stigmata, etc., it is
praiseworthy to desire and ask for what is essential to
this life, namely passive union with God and the sense of

[1] Cf. *Journal Spirituel de Lucie-Christine*, p. 261. *Anthologie Mystique*,
p. 332.

His loving presence within us. Evidently we must ask for that favour with great humility, recognising our complete unworthiness of such a grace. We need not add that such a request presupposes a generous soul, ready to die to self and all things.

If God in His gratuitous liberality has already favoured us with this grace, nothing prevents us desiring to receive it more and more frequently. But let us always leave the choice of time and manner to our Lord. He will mould us according to His divine plan and knows better than we what is good for us. What matter whether the sense of God's presence be vivid or almost imperceptible, arid or pleasurable, whether it affects our emotions or is confined to the most spiritual part of the soul. We must always gratefully receive such a precious means of advancing in union with Jesus and of faithfully attending lovingly to Him. The great point is not to desire these favours for their own sake, for the pleasure and delight they may give, but solely as means to union with God. We must always love God in and above His gifts.

We must not be upset if, perhaps, after showering us with gifts, the Divine Master seems to hide Himself for a long time, perhaps even for years. Let us try to keep intact our trust in His infinite Goodness. Above all, we must never be discouraged. The soul that is passing through the terrible night of the spirit has no longer any idea what Jesus' beloved presence is. That precious sentiment has given place to a painful sense of His absence. But this painful absence and terrible night is itself a great grace which wonderfully purifies the soul to her very depths and thus prepares her for the longed-for ultimate, perfect transforming union.

32. SUB SPECIE AETERNITATIS[1]

1. Our life on earth ought to be a long journey towards the life of heaven and a gradual preparation for it. We ought even now to make ourselves familiar with the sentiments which will be our happiness for all eternity. If, therefore, we really understand the spiritual life, we will gradually accustom ourselves to look at all things, with the eyes of living faith, as God and the saints in heaven see them, and to love them as they do, and as we will in eternity. That is, we will see only God in everything, love Him alone and in everything. Such is the essential of the life of a soul closely united to God.

In proportion as the soul thus comes to see and love all things as God sees and loves them, sub specie aeternitatis, in the light of eternity, she builds up an ever larger store of joyous serene peace, and imperturbable calm, which is a foretaste of heaven.

2. No doubt this earth is a vale of tears. It is a stage on which appear in turn all sorts of vices, human miseries, and sufferings. Even though we see so little of all this, we are sometimes overwhelmed, almost discouraged, at the sight of so much evil, iniquity and suffering. We might sometimes be tempted to say to ourselves, ''What satisfaction can God find in such a wretched world? Why didn't He create a world free from all physical and moral evil, and which would have glorified Him a thousand times better?'' Yet we see only a little corner of the earth. What would it be if we saw the whole world from on high, as God and the saints see it, from whom no detail of these miseries is hidden?

Yet from the height of heaven, God and His saints

[1]From the point of view of Eternity.

contemplate with perfect serenity and ineffable bliss the world which pursues its course under their eyes, with all its wickedness and suffering. Far from being saddened at what afflicts us and fills us with dismay, the elect bless and praise God unreservedly.

This world, full of revolting wickedness and filth, appears to them shining in the rays of the divine perfections. They grasp the history of the world in one inclusive glance and see in it the wonderful manifestation of infinite Wisdom, Beauty, Holiness, Love, Justice, Power and Mercy. In their eyes the world is as it were an immense prism through which the white light of the divine essence is refracted and shines in a wonderful radiance of divine attributes. They see in it the perfect realisation of God's eternal plan, and they are thereby filled with a joy, gratitude and ecstasy of love which will last throughout eternity, untroubled for ever by the slightest shadow of sadness or regret.

3. If only we could see the world and our own life with all its varied details and different events, a little as the elect see them, how happy we should be! Nothing would upset us, for we should see how everything works for good for those who love God. Diligentibus Deum omnia cooperantur in bonum (Rom. viii. 28). Behind the innumerable created causes that criss-cross and form the texture of our life, we would always perceive the First Cause active in everything, operating in all things gently but firmly, working with untiring love for our sanctification and eternal happiness.

That is the secret of the wonderful peace that even in this life fills souls perfectly united to God, the souls of saints. Like their heavenly brothers and sisters, they see in everything the perfect accomplishment of the divine plan, and through all the vicissitudes of life their hearts

ceaselessly breathe out hymns of praise and benediction.
Bene fecit omnia. He has done all things well.

Having arrived, after a difficult ascent, at the summit
of the spiritual life, holy people enjoy a wonderful view.
They have left far below them the harsh noises and
tumult of the earth and are now bathed in the calm of
the peaks raised far above the clouds and storms that
rage at their feet.

4. Even the great catastrophes that stand out in the
history of the world, even the great and disconcerting
disasters that have befallen the Church, the terrible per-
secutions and even more terrible heresies that have
carried away innumerable multitudes like a devastating
flood, the schisms which have torn and rent the Church's
unity, everything appears to them as part of the eternal
plan of God, irradiated with heavenly light. Many things
no doubt remain mysterious to them. They have not the
clear vision of heaven. They only see by the luminous
obscurity of living faith, but its mysterious light is
sufficient to give their souls deep peace, a habitual and
lively awareness that despite appearances God puts into
effect in everything His incomparable work of love and
mercy.

That is why St. Ignatius of Loyola, for example, despite
the ardent zeal that devoured him, and the great love he
had for his Society, could say that if ever it pleased God
to allow the Society to be destroyed, a quarter of an
hour's prayer would suffice to console him for so
immense a ruin.

Souls who have achieved perfect union with God see
the whole world as a magnificent painting by the Divine
Master, in which there is a reason for every detail and
in which light and shade contribute to the beauty of the
whole.

Or they view it as a tremendous symphony composed of infinitely varied instruments and voices, the unique and universal symphony in which each created thing has its part, the wonderful symphony in which Christ with His mystical body, the tens of millions of men who belong to Him and are animated by His life and love, glorify the Father in the incomparable harmony that will be our eternal admiration in heaven.

Moreover, the experience of her own life only strengthens this trustful peace in a soul united to God. She has passed through many various stages, known many successes and failures, enjoyed the delight of many spiritual consolations as well as the bitterness of desolation and trials, some of them terrible ones. Gradually she has come to realise by experience that, through everything, God's loving plan for her is always carried out, in a hidden way perhaps, but with certainty. "Misericordias Domini cantabo in aeternum" (Ps. 88. 2). "I shall sing for ever the mercies of the Lord," she can happily say when she glances over the past. Her life has come to resemble a fine calm evening, fresh and brilliant, with delightful radiance, following on the burning heat of the day or the din and thunder of a storm.

5. Here as always union of the soul with God explains everything. Jesus' life in her is the ultimate reason for her calm and joy, prelude to the life of heaven. It is because each day Jesus lives more fully and freely in her that the soul is more and more conscious of the divine action in her and in the world, and sees more clearly that the divine plan is always wonderfully and infallibly carried into effect. In reality it is He in her who, by means of the soul's ardent faith vivified by the gifts of the Holy Ghost, contemplates all things and sees behind all second causes God, whose wisdom and merciful love is tirelessly

active giving Himself to us to unite us to Him. It is Jesus who gives the soul something of the perfect serenity with which He directs all earthly events.

6. That is not to say that the soul united to God and living in Him always equally enjoys this joyous peace and calm springing from her awareness of God's plan, or becomes indifferent to earthly sufferings and misfortunes. Far from it. The soul is still on earth, her ship has not yet cast anchor in the harbour of eternity. She still remains to some extent tossed by the angry waves of the sea of this life, and by changes in the spiritual life. At times the light within is more brilliant, Jesus' action and life make themselves more felt. At other times she is a prey to aridity, and desolation, and vividly feels once more the distress caused by the difficulties of her apostolate, the sight of so much wickedness and suffering. In this way she passes from a state of deep peace in which all human sorrow loses its bitterness for her, to a state of desolation at the things of earth. Gradually, however, she tends to fix her abode in the serene happy kingdom of peace of which the Apostle spoke. Pax super omnem sensum—Peace that surpasses all understanding.

May we one day be numbered, thanks to our growing union with God, among the blessed souls in whom Christ lives fully, and who even on earth see all things to some extent as God and the saints see them, sub specie aeternitatis, from the point of view of eternity. Never to be upset, whatever happens, never to be dismayed, always unshakably to believe in the excess of divine love that rules our life, that is a happiness we could never desire too earnestly, never ask of God too insistently, the best of all preparations for the changelessly happy life of eternity.